Fast Ed's
DINNER IN 10

Cook simple, stylish food in 10 minutes *flat*!

Ed Halmagyi

EBURY PRESS

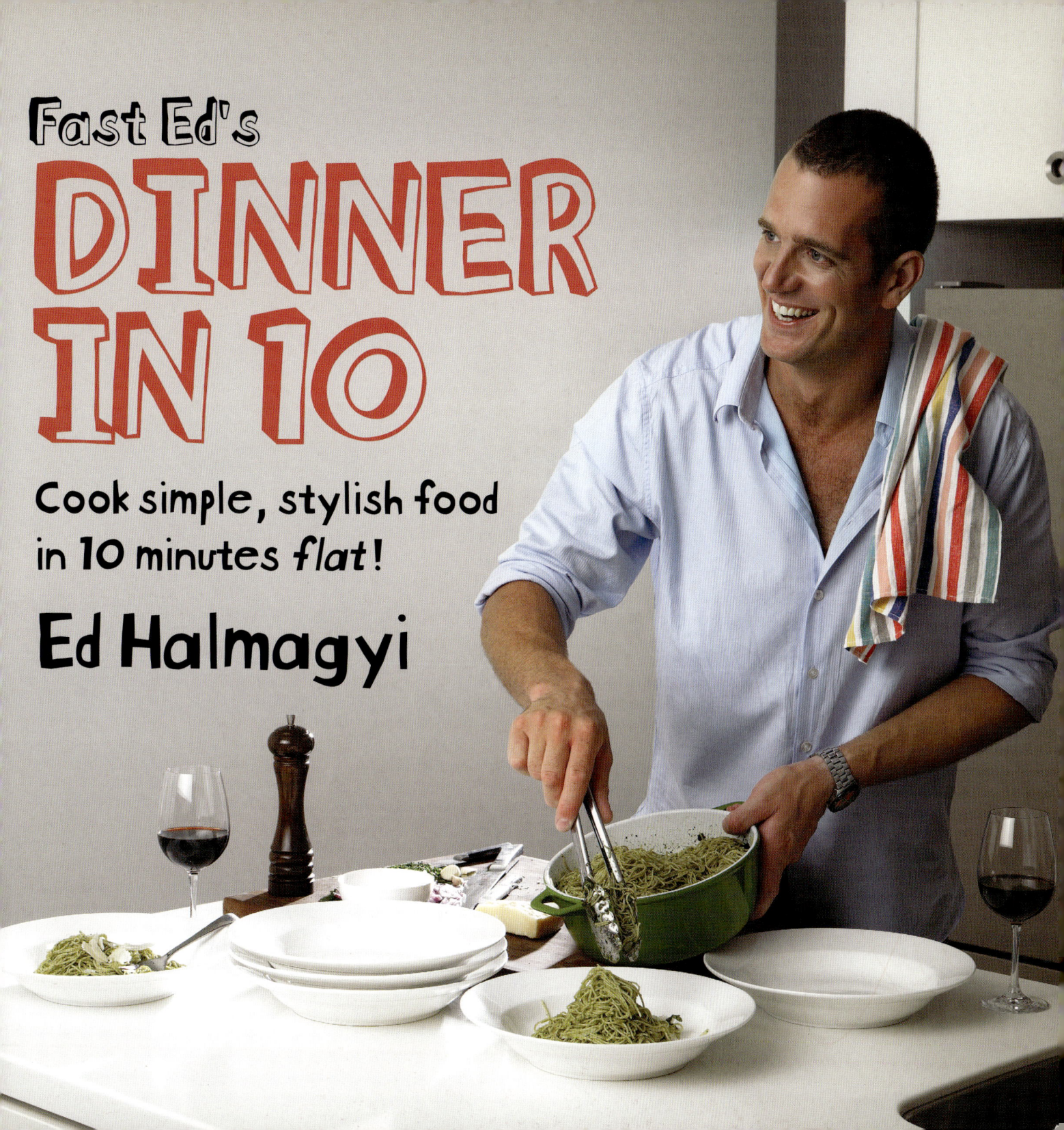

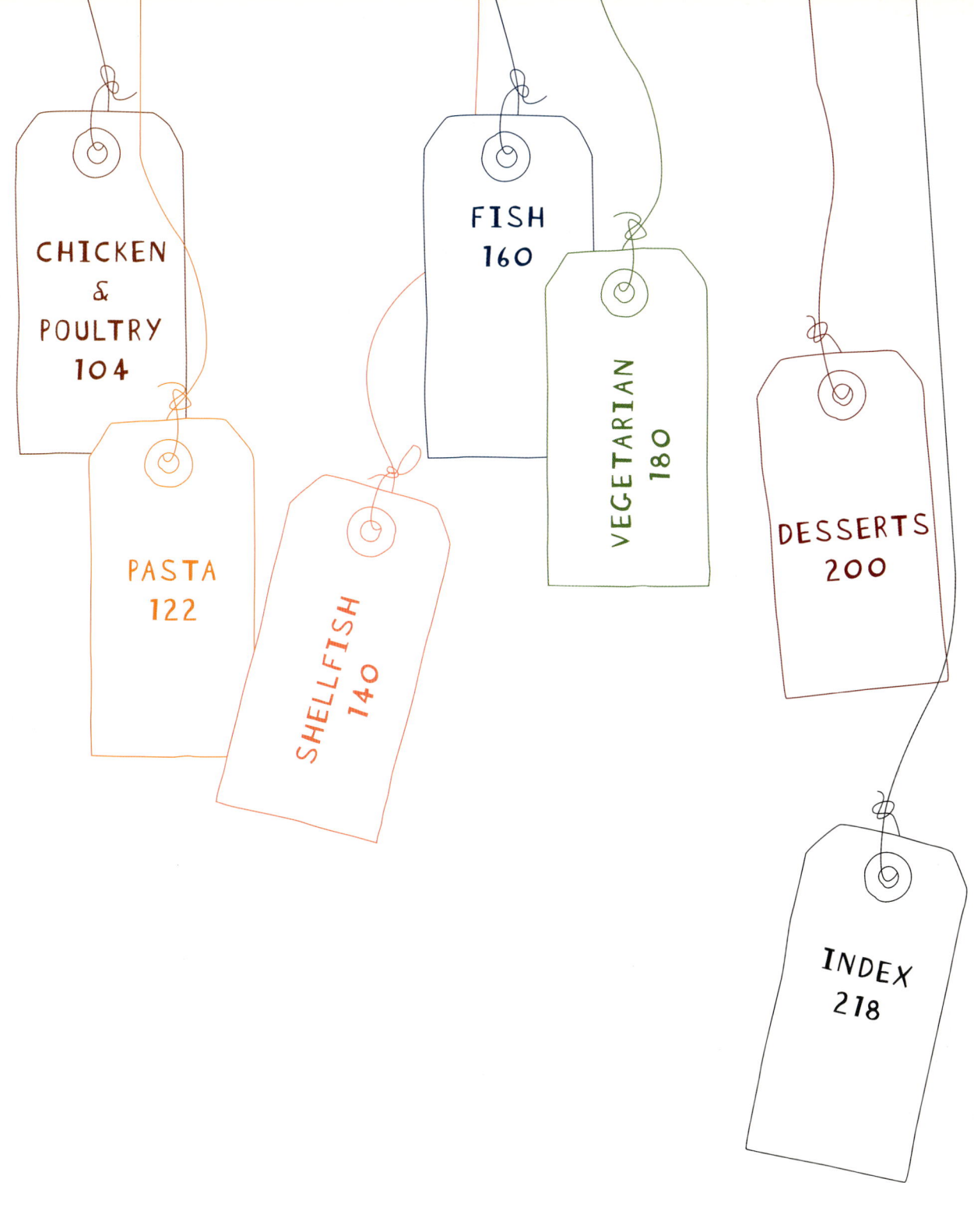

INTRODUCTION

I don't receive many dinner invitations.

That probably sounds like a poor reflection on my social skills or my table manners, but I'm pretty sure that's not the case. We eat out with friends regularly, and I'll always happily have them over to our place. It's just that preparing a home-cooked dinner doesn't seem to appeal to my mates. It's not that they lack the capacity. Actually, they're all creative people who can turn their hand to most art forms, so I'm sure they could manage cooking.

Nope. The more I think about it the more I'm convinced that there are two big problems at the heart of the issue: confidence and information.

A crisis of confidence seems to arise from mistaken expectations. Put simply, most folks don't want to cook for chefs. Panic sets in because surely someone who cooks professionally every day could never be content eating a meal without a star rating. I'd never really put much stock by this concern until I saw it for myself.

A close friend named John (name kept exactly the same to maximise public humiliation) had always struck me as the classic Renaissance man: erudite, athletic and charming to a fault. So, who then was the wild-eyed and dishevelled creature I found in his kitchen, beaded with sweat and cursing the oven? 'Why did we have to invite the bloody chef?' he muttered to himself. I withdrew quietly and went unnoticed back to the lounge room.

As it turned out dinner was fine, if overly complicated, although John seemed to savour neither the success of his own generosity nor the raucous satisfaction of his guests. He was like a final year student desperately awaiting the examiner's verdict. He had bundled all his culinary anxieties into an exaggerated aversion to having a cooking professional at the table. The similar anxieties of our other friends seems to account for why we don't get asked out that much. However, I suspect there's a bit more to it.

I reckon most people fear cooking for groups almost as much as they loathe public speaking. Like oratory, it has something to do with the solitariness of the task, and how it exposes us to judgement. Our food is a reflection of ourselves, and so we infer a great deal from the discerning assessments of our guests. Having a chef to dinner just amplifies those fears of failure.

Sound familiar? Well, it needn't be.

Let me share with you a crucial lesson from the world of high-end restaurants. It's the kind of secret spoken in hushed tones by the individuals in really tall hats as they gently stir the soup.

The food is only part of the job. One part. An important part, but by no means the only one.

What you serve and how you prepare it may define your experience as host, but for the guests dining is equally to do with ambience, wine, laughter and conversation. Great hosts should position themselves to provide all those elements all at once. Don't be overwhelmed by the idea of cooking; entertaining is much harder than that!

So, as I sat back in my chair and surveyed the scene at John's party, I understood what was missing. It was John. In his frail and traumatised post-cooking state, he lacked the strength to chat or the capacity to laugh. All he wanted was a stiff drink. It was such a waste of his vibrant personality. As a dinner guest he's usually the life of the party.

What then of cooking for chefs? Well, this is the bit you're going to love. I spend my days tasting my own food at length. I have a keen sense of what I like, and I have honed my skills over the years. I don't mind saying that I'm pretty good at my craft. But do you know what I crave most? Do you know which meal I enjoy best?

The one I don't have to cook.

I am still passionately excited by cookery and all its processes. I marvel at the transformation ingredients undergo as we transport them from the paddock to the plate. And I delight in the unalloyed pleasure of having a meal arrive complete, manufactured by another hand, while I remain blissfully ignorant of its odyssey to my table.

In short, I love being a guest. All good chefs do. You can never conquer the challenge of providing hospitality unless you can empathise with the experience of those you serve. Or maybe it's just that I love having the night off.

Once your confidence is sorted, the other part of the cookery conundrum is information, getting the formulas right. For this, you need recipes that are elegant and impressive yet achievable in the face of distraction. Whether you are cooking a simple weekday family meal or a lavish party for friends, the principle remains the same. You are supposed to be part of the action, so you want recipes that deliver quality but get you out of the kitchen in good time.

Here's an important observation: more dinners are ruined by overexertion than by sloth. You may have heard that less is more, but how do you put that into practice in your cooking? Consider a shift to simplicity.

As an extremely talented Frenchman once explained to me, 'Beautiful food is like a great romance. Do not pursue too much, let her come to you.' Choose good-quality ingredients; they will always serve you well. If you start with good flavour, you will reduce the need for complex technique considerably. But the same lesson applies in reverse. Once you have assembled quality components resist the temptation to overreach your culinary skills. When you do less, the ingredients can do more.

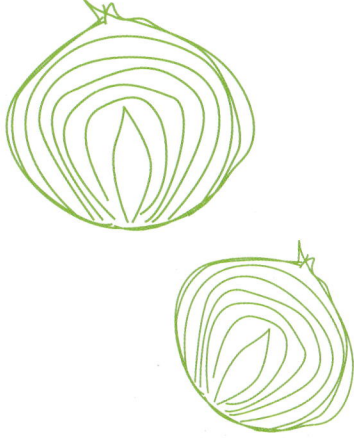

So all in all, this was the reason for *Dinner in 10*. It's a purpose-driven resource that helps you to enjoy your cooking more by getting you out of the kitchen more quickly. I have tested and re-tested every recipe using only domestic equipment, and have cooked on both electric and gas stoves. I know that these recipes work.

But you must maintain a measure of perspective when you embark on this journey with me. Your first attempt will not be your best, and it may take you a couple of tries to get comfortable with the different approach I've taken in the methods I've devised.

The countdown from 10 to 1 marks the minute intervals to help you serve dinner in just 10 minutes, so get used to using a clock. But also remember that you have to be flexible. Your pan may not have been hot enough at the start, or your butcher may have cut the steaks too thick. Perhaps the phone rings and your timing goes awry. Keep cool and stay focused. Rest assured this new cooking technique will help you, but, like learning to ride a bike, you may have a few spills along the way.

I've written this book for all the people who become nervous at the prospect of cooking, and for everyone who has written to me to say that fast food is just a myth. I can do it and, more importantly, so can you. Just follow the five rules over the page, and have some fun. Soon you'll have no hesitation in asking chefs to your place to sample your wares!

INTRODUCTION

THE RULES

1 Start with a clean kitchen. When you want to cook, especially when you want to cook quickly, you need as much space as possible. So pack away any appliances that aren't needed, put the kids' school papers in a drawer, and give the bench a good wipe down. A clean, clear space will improve your speed and increase your enjoyment of the cooking process.

2 Lay out all the equipment and the ingredients before you start.

3 Read the recipe before you get going, twice. If you have any questions look them up before you start cooking.

4 Motivation is the key to success, so cook with purpose and energy. You only have 10 minutes, so keep your speed up. The idea is to get in and out of the kitchen as fast as possible, so you have more time to sit and enjoy your creation!

5 Substitution's fine, provided you know what you're doing. Keep in mind that changes to ingredients may affect the cooking time.

✻ All recipes serve 4.

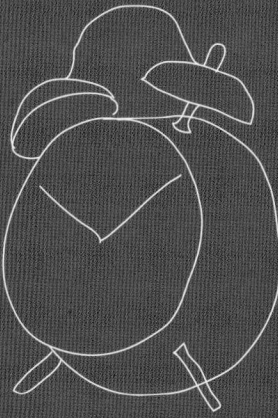

For Noodle and Moo.
The best reason to cook quickly.

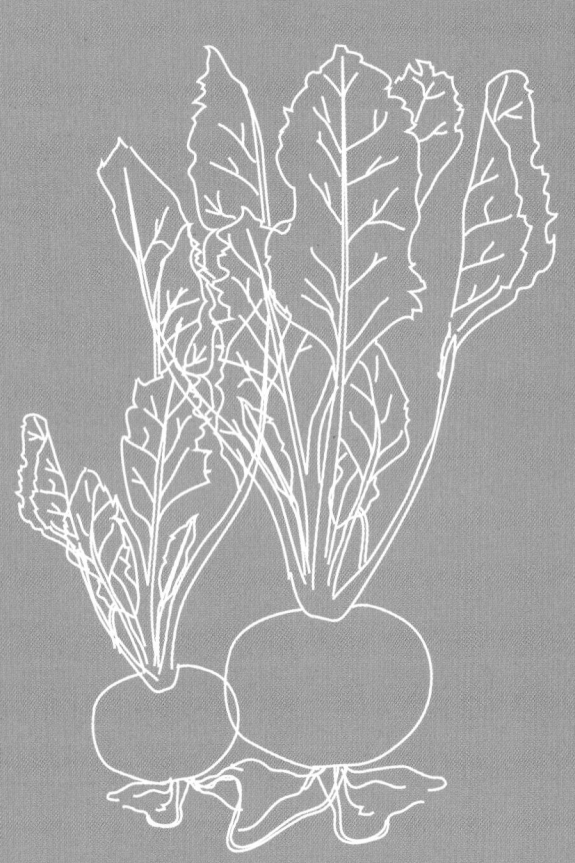

SOUP

CHICKEN AND CORN MISO BROTH WITH SCALLOPS AND ALMONDS

FIRST
warm 4 serving bowls

GEAR
5L saucepan
wooden spoon
chopping board
knife
frying pan
ladle

FOOD
1 skinless chicken thigh fillet
2 tsp sesame oil
4 pickled onions
1 bunch coriander
½ tsp minced ginger
1 Tbsp white miso paste
1½L liquid chicken stock
400g can corn kernels
½ cup green beans
1 long red chilli
salt and pepper
12 scallops, roe removed
2 tsp sliced almonds

10 Set the 5L saucepan over a high heat. Slice the chicken thigh finely.

9 Pour the sesame oil into the saucepan and add the chicken. Stir well. Slice the pickled onions and transfer to the saucepan.

8 Roughly chop the coriander roots, then pick the leaves and set aside. Add the coriander roots, ginger and miso paste to the saucepan and stir well.

7 Pour the chicken stock into the saucepan, stir well, and allow to come to the boil. Drain and rinse the corn kernels.

6 Slice the green beans finely. Stir the saucepan.

5 Slice the long red chilli finely. Stir the saucepan.

4 Set the frying pan over a high heat. Add the corn and green beans to the saucepan.

3 Season the soup with salt and pepper, then ladle into the warmed bowls.

2 Sear the scallops in a very hot frying pan with no oil for 15 seconds each side until just browned. Arrange the scallops in the centre of the soup.

1 Garnish the soup with sliced almonds, chilli and reserved coriander leaves.

Miso paste is a wonderfully versatile Japanese ingredient, made from fermented soy beans. It is a flavour paste found in most supermarkets, used to make soups much like traditional stocks. In this recipe I use the miso to enrich the already flavoursome chicken stock.

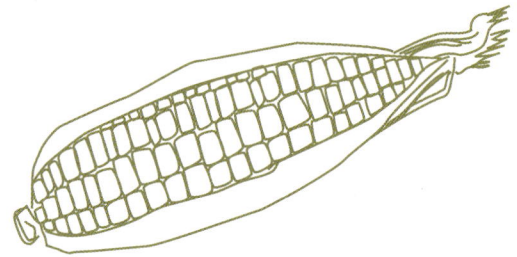

CREAMY PARSNIP SOUP WITH WHOLEWHEAT CROUTONS AND OREGANO RELISH

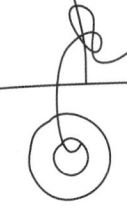

The speed in this recipe comes from slicing the vegetables as finely as possible. If you lack confidence in your knife skills, invest in a mandoline slicer. You'll find them at all kitchenware stores.

FIRST
boil 1L water in kettle
warm 4 serving bowls

GEAR
5L saucepan
wooden spoon
knife
vegetable peeler
chopping board
toaster
mortar and pestle
stick blender

FOOD
1 brown onion
500g parsnips
3 cloves garlic
2 Tbsp vegetable oil
salt and pepper
1 slice wholewheat bread
2 chicken stock cubes
1L boiling water
300ml thickened cream
1 bunch oregano leaves
1 tsp capers
1 lemon, zest and juice
3 Tbsp extra virgin olive oil

10 Set the 5L saucepan over a high heat. Peel the onion, parsnips and garlic.

9 Slice the onion and parsnips finely. Crush the garlic with a knife.

8 Pour the vegetable oil into the pan and add the vegetables and garlic, then stir well. Season lightly with salt and pepper. Place the bread in a toaster and cook to dark golden.

7 Crumble the stock cubes into the pan, stir well and cook for 1 minute.

6 Add the boiling water to the pan and stir well to ensure that any caramelised vegetables are released from the base. Continue simmering.

5 Add the cream to the pan, stir well, and bring the mixture to a rapid boil. Place the oregano, capers and lemon zest in the mortar and pound firmly.

4 Turn the heat under the pan to low. Continue pounding the oregano relish until it forms a smooth, dark green paste.

3 Stir the lemon juice and olive oil into the oregano mixture, then season with salt and pepper. Remove the crusts from the toasted bread and dice into 1cm cubes.

2 Puree the soup with the stick blender until very smooth, then adjust the seasoning to taste.

1 Pour the soup into the warmed bowls, drizzle with oregano relish and top with croutons.

SOUP

PEA AND HAM SOUP, EXCEPT THAT MY WIFE'S A VEGETARIAN!

FIRST
defrost the peas
warm 4 serving bowls

GEAR
5L saucepan
chopping board
knife
frying pan
mixing bowl
ladle

FOOD
1 brown onion
200g sliced ham off the bone
½ bunch thyme
2 tsp baby capers
1 Tbsp mustard seed oil
1 tsp vegetable oil
1 medium gherkin
2 tsp minced horseradish
1½L liquid vegetable stock
salt and pepper
500g frozen peas, defrosted
4 slices crusty bread
1 cup milk
½ bunch oregano leaves

10 Set the 5L saucepan over a high heat and the frying pan over a medium heat. Peel the onion and dice finely. Slice the ham into fine strips. Chop the thyme.

9 Place the onion, capers, thyme and mustard seed oil in the saucepan and stir well. Sprinkle the ham into the frying pan and add the vegetable oil. Stir well.

8 Finely dice the gherkin and stir into the saucepan. Stir the ham.

7 Add the horseradish to the saucepan, stir well and cook for 30 seconds.

6 Pour the vegetable stock into the saucepan, season with salt and pepper, then bring to the boil. Stir the ham and reduce the heat under the frying pan to low.

5 Add the peas to the saucepan, stir well and simmer.

4 Tear the bread into chunks and place in the mixing bowl. Pour the milk over the bread and set aside for the bread to absorb the milk. Stir the ham.

3 Once the ham is crisp, drain on absorbent paper and set aside. Pick the oregano leaves.

2 Squeeze the excess milk from the bread and divide among the warmed bowls.

1 Ladle the soup over the bread and garnish with oregano leaves and ham chips (for the carnivores!).

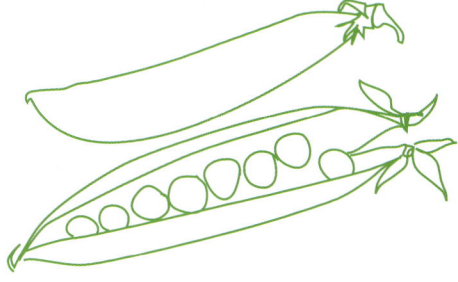

LETTUCE AND WATERCRESS SOUP WITH CRISPY ONIONS

Baby cos lettuce is a great substitute for the butter lettuce with an equally big flavour.

FIRST
boil 2L water in kettle
warm 4 serving bowls

GEAR
5L saucepan
3L saucepan
wooden spoon
tongs
colander
deep frying pan
blender
knife
chopping board
large mixing bowl
large plastic bag
slotted spoon

FOOD
2L boiling water
2 tsp bicarbonate of soda
1 head butter lettuce
1 bunch watercress
1 bunch flat-leaf parsley
700ml bottle Riesling
1L liquid vegetable stock
1 leek
1 brown onion
vegetable oil, for frying
1 Tbsp Worcestershire sauce
½ tsp ground nutmeg
½ tsp ground cumin
½ cup milk
1 cup self-raising flour
2 tsp Cajun seasoning
salt and pepper

10 Set the 3L saucepan over a high heat, then add the boiling water and bicarbonate of soda. Tear the leaves off the lettuce and immerse them in the boiling water for 20 seconds, then remove with a pair of tongs and set to drain in a colander. Set the 5L saucepan over a high heat.

9 Trim the bulk of the stalks from the watercress and parsley. Dip the leafy sections in the boiling water for 30 seconds, then drain in the colander.

8 Pour the wine and stock into the 5L saucepan and bring to the boil. Cut the leek into fine slices. Add to the wine mixture.

7 Add the lettuce, watercress and parsley to the wine mixture and bring to a high simmer. Adjust the temperature to keep the mixture simmering.

6 Stir the lettuce mixture well. Peel the onion and slice into 1cm discs. Separate the discs to make onion rings.

5 Pour the vegetable oil into the frying pan and set over a high heat.

4 Add the Worcestershire sauce and spices to the lettuce mixture and stir well. Dip the onion rings in milk. Place the flour and Cajun seasoning in the plastic bag, then drain the onion rings and add them to the bag. Shake well to ensure all the rings are well coated.

3 Pour the soup into the blender and puree until very smooth. Shake the excess flour off the rings and place them in the hot oil then fry until crisp.

2 Season the soup with salt and pepper. Drain the crispy onions on absorbent paper.

1 Pour the soup into the warmed bowls and garnish with a pile of onion rings.

HOT AND SOUR DUCK SOUP WITH SHALLOTS AND MINT

FIRST
boil 1L water in kettle
warm 4 serving bowls

GEAR
wok
wooden spoon
chopping board
knife
mixing bowl
whisk
ladle

FOOD
¼ Chinese BBQ duck
¼ bunch shallots
1 punnet shiitake mushrooms
5cm piece ginger
2 tsp sesame oil
200g can bamboo shoots
2 red birdseye chillies
100g firm tofu
¼ bunch mint
2 chicken stock cubes
1L boiling water
3 Tbsp dark soy sauce
2 Tbsp white vinegar
salt and white pepper
2 eggs
2 tsp chilli oil

10 Shred the duck meat, including skin, into fine pieces, reserving the bones. Slice the white part of the shallots, reserving the green part.

9 Set the wok over a high heat. Slice the shiitake mushrooms and the ginger finely.

8 Pour the sesame oil into the wok then add the duck meat, white slices of shallots, mushrooms and ginger. Stir well. Drain and rinse the bamboo shoots, then slice finely and add to the wok.

7 Stir the wok well. Slice the chillies finely and dice the tofu, then set aside.

6 Pick the mint leaves and slice the green parts of the shallots and set aside. Stir the wok well.

5 Add the stock cubes, boiling water, soy sauce and vinegar to the wok and stir well. Add the reserved duck bones. Bring it to the boil.

4 Add the tofu and chillies to the wok and reduce the heat to low. Stir gently.

3 Season the soup lightly with salt and white pepper. Break the eggs into a mixing bowl and whisk well. Remove the duck bones from the wok.

2 Stir the soup gently in a circular motion then add the egg in a steady stream.

1 Ladle the soup into the warmed bowls and garnish with mint leaves, green slices of shallots and chilli oil.

BORSCHT ON THE RUN

FIRST
boil 500ml water in kettle
warm 4 serving bowls

GEAR
5L saucepan
wooden spoon
knife
chopping board
vegetable peeler
colander
box grater
scissors

FOOD
2 rashers rindless bacon
1 leek
2 Tbsp mustard seed oil
1 stick celery
2 cloves garlic, peeled
1 large Desiree potato
salt and pepper
2 x 340g cans whole baby beetroot
500ml boiling water
1 chicken stock cube
4 Tbsp sour cream
½ bunch chives
crusty bread, to serve

10 Set the 5L saucepan over a high heat. Slice the bacon finely. Cut away the green part of the leek and finely slice the white part only.

9 Place the leek in a colander, then rinse lightly to remove any dirt.

8 Place the bacon and leek in the pan with the mustard seed oil, then stir well. Slice the celery and garlic finely. Peel the potato.

7 Continue cooking the bacon mixture, stirring often, until it begins to caramelise and turn golden brown. Grate the potato coarsely and add it to the pan.

6 Add the celery and garlic to the pan and stir thoroughly. Season generously with salt and pepper, and stir well.

5 Drain the cans of beetroot, reserving half the liquid. Grate the beetroot coarsely and add to the pan.

4 Pour in the beetroot juice and the boiling water and crumble in the stock cube. Bring to the boil.

3 Reduce the heat to medium and continue simmering, stirring occasionally.

2 Snip the chives into fine batons using scissors.

1 Pour the soup into the warmed bowls and spoon some sour cream into the centre of each. Garnish with chives and serve with crusty bread.

Baby beetroot—not the sliced variety—are preserved in a less vinegary solution, which makes the soup a lot more tasty.

SOUP

SOUPY GOULASH OF SAUSAGE AND CAPSICUMS

FIRST
boil 1L water in kettle
warm 4 serving bowls

GEAR
5L saucepan
chopping board
knife
wooden spoon
ladle

FOOD
1 brown onion
1 clove garlic
1 Tbsp unsalted butter
4 pork sausages
120g rindless smoked speck
1 green capsicum
1 Tbsp Hungarian sweet paprika
1 tsp caraway seeds
½ tsp ground fennel seeds
1 Tbsp tomato paste
150g peeled roasted red capsicums
2 beef stock cubes
1L boiling water
salt and pepper
½ bunch flat-leaf parsley
100g sour cream

10 Set the 5L saucepan over a high heat. Peel the onion and slice it finely. Peel the garlic and crush lightly with a knife.

9 Place the butter in the pan and add the onion and garlic. Stir well. Cut the sausages into 2cm pieces. Dice the speck finely.

8 Add the sausages and speck to the pan. Stir well. Dice the green capsicum finely.

7 Add the spices to the pan and stir well until the mixture becomes aromatic. Add the tomato paste and continue cooking until the mixture begins to stick to the bottom of the pan. Slice the roasted red capsicums finely.

6 Add both capsicums to the pan and stir well.

5 Crumble the stock cubes into the pan and stir well to incorporate, then add the boiling water. Bring to the boil.

4 Stir well.

3 Reduce the heat to low and stir well. Season with salt and a generous amount of pepper.

2 Chop the parsley finely.

1 Ladle the soup into the warmed bowls and garnish with sour cream and chopped parsley.

Speck is an Austrian ham flavoured with juniper berries. It is also very popular in Hungarian cookery. You'll find it at all good delicatessens. While you're at the deli counter, grab some marinated roasted red capsicums, they are usually more flavour-some than the bottled or canned varieties.

OYSTER CHOWDER WITH KIDNEY BEANS AND SNOWPEAS

FIRST
warm 4 serving bowls

GEAR
5L saucepan
chopping board
knife
wooden spoon
ladle

FOOD
1 brown onion
2 cloves garlic
2 sticks celery
1 large washed potato
2 anchovy fillets
2 Tbsp unsalted butter
400g snapper or other white fish
2 dozen shucked oysters
2 Tbsp plain flour
2 Tbsp brandy
1L liquid fish stock
500ml liquid chicken stock
salt and white pepper
150ml double cream
400g can kidney beans
1 cup snowpeas
½ bunch flat-leaf parsley

10 Set the 5L saucepan over a high heat. Peel the onion and dice roughly. Peel the garlic and crush lightly with a knife.

9 Dice the celery sticks. Peel the potato and dice. Add the onion, garlic, celery, potato, anchovies and butter to the pan and stir well.

8 Dice the fish, remove the oysters from their shells, and set aside. Stir the pan.

7 Stir the flour into the pan and cook for 30 seconds. Stir in the brandy.

6 Add the stocks, fish and oysters and stir well. Allow to come to the boil.

5 Season the soup with salt and pepper, then add the cream and stir well.

4 Drain and rinse the kidney beans. Top and tail the snowpeas and slice finely. Stir the pan.

3 Add the kidney beans to the pan and stir thoroughly.

2 Stir in the snowpeas. Chop the parsley finely.

1 Ladle the soup into the warmed bowls and garnish with the parsley.

SPINACH SOUP WITH ARTICHOKE AND GORGONZOLA TOASTS

Choose artichoke hearts in oil, not vinegar, for flavour and texture.

FIRST
boil 2L water in kettle
warm 4 serving bowls

GEAR
5L saucepan
3L saucepan
ribbed skillet
wooden spoon
chopping board
knife
colander
small mixing bowl
blender
ladle

FOOD
1 leek
1 clove garlic
¼ cup pitted green olives
2 anchovy fillets
¼ tsp ground fenugreek
2 Tbsp avocado oil
2L boiling water
2 bunches English spinach
1 bunch flat-leaf parsley
2 tsp cornflour
1L vegetable stock
2 Tbsp double cream
2 artichoke hearts
1 eschalot
2 Tbsp gorgonzola cheese
salt and pepper
½ baguette
2 Tbsp extra virgin olive oil
4 Tbsp Greek yoghurt

10 Set the 5L saucepan and the 3L saucepan over high heat, and set the ribbed skillet over a medium heat. Cut away the green part of the leek then finely slice the white part only, then rinse lightly in a colander to remove any dirt. Peel the garlic clove and crush lightly with a knife.

9 Place the leek, garlic, olives, anchovy, fenugreek and avocado oil in the 5L saucepan and stir well. Pour the boiling water into the 3L saucepan.

8 Tear off the spinach and parsley leaves and immerse in the boiling water for 30 seconds, then drain in the colander and refresh under cold running water. Stir the leek mixture.

7 Add the cornflour to the leek mixture and stir well. Cook for 20 seconds then add the vegetable stock and double cream and stir thoroughly. Bring to the boil.

6 Reduce the heat under the 5L saucepan to low and add the spinach and parsley leaves. Simmer gently.

5 Dice the artichoke finely. Stir the spinach mixture.

4 Peel the eschalot and slice finely. Combine eschalot, artichoke and gorgonzola in a small mixing bowl, then set aside.

3 Pour the spinach mixture into a blender and puree until very smooth. Season with salt and pepper. Slice the baguette into four long bias-cut strips.

2 Brush the baguette with olive oil and toast quickly in the ribbed skillet until lightly blackened. Spoon the artichoke mixture onto the toasts.

1 Ladle the soup into the warmed bowls and place a spoon of yoghurt in the centre. Lay a baguette toast on the side of each bowl.

SMOKED CHICKEN, SWEET POTATO AND COCONUT GUMBO

Look out for spiced sunflower seeds in your local health food store or make your own by frying sunflower seeds in Cajun spices, a little salt and some light olive oil until crisp.

FIRST
warm 4 serving bowls

GEAR
5L saucepan
chopping board
knife
colander
wooden spoon
vegetable peeler
small mixing bowl
ladle

FOOD
½ leek
100g hot Spanish salami
2 Tbsp olive oil
1 red capsicum
200g sweet potato
½ bunch silverbeet
3 cloves garlic
1 Tbsp Creole seasoning
1 tsp dried thyme leaves
1 Tbsp cornflour
2 Tbsp dark rum
2 chicken stock cubes
700ml white wine
400ml coconut cream
250g smoked chicken
salt and pepper
¼ bunch basil leaves
¼ cup spiced sunflower seeds

10 Set the 5L saucepan over a medium heat. Cut away the green part of the leek, slice the white part only then rinse lightly in a colander to remove any dirt. Dice the salami. Place the leek, salami and olive oil in the saucepan and stir well.

9 Dice the capsicum. Peel the sweet potato and dice finely. Slice the silverbeet stems, reserving the leaves. Add the capsicum, sweet potato and silverbeet stems to the pan.

8 Peel the garlic and crush lightly with a knife. Add garlic to the pan and stir well. Combine the cornflour and rum in the small mixing bowl and set side.

7 Stir in the Creole seasoning and dried thyme, then crumble in the stock cubes.

6 Pour in the white wine and coconut cream then stir thoroughly. Shred the smoked chicken finely.

5 Season with salt and pepper and stir well. Stir in the cornflour mixture.

4 Stir in the shredded chicken and reduce the heat to a simmer. Shred the reserved silverbeet leaves very finely and stir into the pan.

3 Pick the basil leaves. Stir the pan thoroughly.

2 Slice the basil leaves.

1 Ladle the soup into the warmed bowls and garnish with the basil and sunflower seeds.

GAZPACHO FOR A SUMMER DAY

FIRST
chill 4 serving bowls

GEAR
chopping board
knife
large mixing bowl
small mixing bowl
food mill
food processor
ladle

FOOD
2 sticks celery
2 Lebanese cucumbers
4 vine-ripened tomatoes
1 red onion
4 cloves garlic
¼ bunch basil
½ bunch coriander
¼ bunch flat-leaf parsley
1 Tbsp smoked paprika
1 tsp ground cumin seeds
½ tsp ground coriander seeds
salt and pepper
1 Tbsp Worcestershire sauce
2 tsp Tabasco sauce
500ml tomato juice
4 cups ice
crusty bread, to serve

10 Roughly chop the celery, cucumbers and tomato and place in a large mixing bowl. Peel the onion and garlic.

9 Chop the onion and garlic and transfer to the large mixing bowl.

8 Pick the herb leaves, chop roughly, and add to the large mixing bowl. Stir well.

7 Add the spices to the large mixing bowl and season generously with salt and pepper.

6 Combine the Worcestershire, Tabasco and tomato juice in the small mixing bowl.

5 Stir the vegetable mixture well.

4 Begin passing the vegetable mixture through the coarse blade of a food mill. If you don't have a food mill, pulse the mixture in a food processor until it becomes coarse in texture.

3 Finish passing the mixture through the food mill. Stir in the tomato juice mixture.

2 Crush the ice in a food processor.

1 Stir the ice into the soup and ladle into the chilled bowls. Serve with crusty bread.

POTAGE OF CELERY WITH SPICY SAUSAGE AND PRAWNS

FIRST
boil 1L water in kettle
warm 4 serving bowls

GEAR
5L saucepan
wooden spoon
chopping board
knife
box grater
large frying pan
blender

FOOD
4 spring onions
1 bunch celery
2 Tbsp unsalted butter
4 cloves garlic, peeled
1 large potato
1 Tbsp extra virgin olive oil
1 chorizo sausage
400g prawn meat
1–2 vegetable stock cubes
1L boiling water
300ml thickened cream
salt and pepper
½ bunch dill
2 tsp chilli oil

10 Set the 5L saucepan over a high heat. Roughly chop the spring onions and celery.

9   Add the butter, spring onions and celery to the saucepan and stir well. Crush the garlic with a knife then stir into the celery mixture.

8   Grate the potato on the coarse blade of a box grater and add to the saucepan. Stir well and continue cooking. Set the frying pan over a high heat and add the olive oil.

7   Slice the sausage finely and add to the frying pan. Add the prawns to the frying pan and stir well. Stir the saucepan.

6   Crumble the stock cubes into the saucepan then stir well. Pour in the boiling water and cream, stir, then allow to come to the boil. Stir the sausage mixture in the frying pan and reduce the heat to medium.

5   Once the soup comes to the boil, reduce the heat to medium then stir well.

4   Season the soup lightly with salt and pepper. Stir the sausages and prawns then turn off the heat under the frying pan.

3   Pour the soup into the blender and puree until smooth.

2   Check the seasoning in the soup and adjust as needed. Chop the dill finely.

1   Divide the sausages and prawns among the warmed bowls. Pour the soup over the top and garnish with chopped dill and chilli oil.

Chorizo is a spicy Spanish-style sausage available at all good delicatessens. It comes in hot and mild varieties.

SMALL BITES

PROSCIUTTO STICKS WIH GRILLED PEAR, HONEY AND WALNUT SALSA

Buy prosciutto sliced fresh to order from the delicatessen as it oxidises quickly after slicing.

GEAR
ribbed griddle
chopping board
vegetable peeler
knife
tongs
small mixing bowl

FOOD
16 fine slices prosciutto
16 Italian breadsticks
2 firm pears
¼ cup walnuts
1 eschalot
¼ bunch mint
1 Tbsp extra virgin olive oil
½ tsp red wine vinegar
salt and pepper
2 Tbsp leatherwood honey

10 Set the ribbed griddle over a medium heat.

9 Using a sharp knife halve the prosciutto slices lengthways.

8 Start wrapping each breadstick with two prosicutto halves.

7 Finish wrapping the breadsticks.

6 Peel the pears, quarter them and remove the stems and seeds.

5 Lay the pear slices on the griddle and cook for 2 minutes until lightly caramelised.

4 Finely chop the walnuts. Peel the eschalot.

3 Finely dice the eschalot, then finely chop the mint. Combine eschalot, mint, walnuts, olive oil and red wine vinegar in the small mixing bowl. Season with salt and pepper.

2 Lay four breadsticks on each serving plate and garnish with two pear quarters drizzled with honey.

1 Garnish with walnut salsa.

CRUMBED CAMEMBERT WITH FENNEL AND PINE NUT SALAD

GEAR
3L saucepan
chopping board
knife
whisk
mandoline slicer
4 medium mixing bowls
1 small mixing bowl
tongs

FOOD
500ml vegetable oil
4 small camembert cheeses
 (100g each)
3 eggs
1 cup plain flour
1 cup breadcrumbs
1 head fennel
½ cup green beans
½ bunch dill
2 Tbsp pine nuts
2 lemons
2 Tbsp avocado oil
1 tsp seeded mustard
salt and pepper

10 Set the 3L saucepan over a medium heat and pour in the vegetable oil. Halve the camembert cheeses. Break the eggs into a medium mixing bowl and whisk well until smooth.

9 Place the flour and breadcrumbs in separate medium mixing bowls. Dip each camembert piece in flour, then egg, then breadcrumbs.

8 Repeat the egg and breadcrumb stages. Set the crumbed camembert pieces aside.

7 Cut out the stem of the fennel using a sharp knife, then shave very finely using a mandoline slicer.

6 Slice the green beans finely.

5 Pick the dill sprigs. Combine the fennel, dill sprigs, green beans and pine nuts in a medium mixing bowl.

4 Halve the lemons and squeeze the juice into the small mixing bowl. Stir in the avocado oil and mustard then season with salt and a generous amount of black pepper.

3 Toss the fennel mixture and lemon dressing together.

2 Fry the crumbed camembert pieces in the hot vegetable oil until golden. Remove with tongs and drain on absorbent paper.

1 Serve a pile of fennel salad next to two halves of fried cheese.

SALMON AND PEA FRITTERS WITH REDCURRANT MAYONNAISE

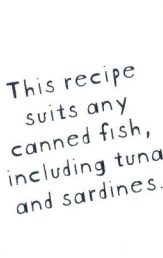

This recipe suits any canned fish, including tuna and sardines.

FIRST
boil 750ml water in kettle

GEAR
1L saucepan
chopping board
knife
large mixing bowl
2 small mixing bowls
frying pan
egg slice

FOOD
750ml boiling water
6 slices white bread
2 eggs
¼ cup buttermilk
200g can red salmon
1 Tbsp sweet chilli sauce
100g frozen peas
salt and pepper
1 cup breadcrumbs
2 Tbsp vegetable oil
3 Tbsp mayonnaise
2 Tbsp redcurrant jelly

10 Set the 1L saucepan over a medium heat and pour in the boiling water. Cut off the crusts from the bread and tear the slices into small pieces. Break the eggs into the large mixing bowl and add the torn bread and buttermilk. Mix well.

9 Drain the can of salmon well. Remove any bones from the salmon.

8 Stir the salmon and sweet chilli sauce into the bread mixture and set aside.

7 Cook the peas in the pan of boiling water for 1 minute then drain and stir into the salmon mixture. Season with salt and pepper then mix well.

6 Place the breadcrumbs into a small mixing bowl.

5 Form the salmon mixture into eight balls. Pour the vegetable oil into the frying pan and set over a medium heat.

4 Roll the salmon balls in breadcrumbs and form into flattened discs.

3 Fry the fritters in vegetable oil on one side until golden.

2 Turn the fritters using the egg slice and cook for 1 more minute until golden on the second side. Combine the mayonnaise and redcurrant jelly.

1 Drain the fritters on absorbent paper and serve with a generous spoon of redcurrant mayonnaise.

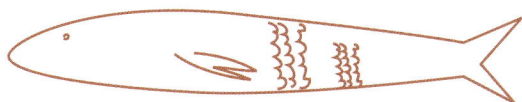

SMALL BITES

TARTARE OF KINGFISH WITH HAZELNUT ROMESCO AND FRIED LEMON

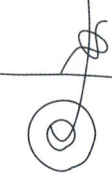

If you have more romesco than you need, store it in an airtight container under a layer of olive oil.

FIRST
choose a big white wine, think nicely wooded Chardonnay

GEAR
large frying pan
chopping board
knife
wooden spoon
food processor
large plate

FOOD
800g boneless kingfish fillet, skin off
200g skinned hazelnut kernels
100g blanched almonds
4 cloves garlic
¼ cup extra virgin olive oil
½ cup breadcrumbs
½ cup roasted red capsicums
¼ cup semi-dried tomatoes
2 tsp smoked paprika
1 tsp ground cumin
salt and pepper
1 lemon
2 Tbsp mustard seed oil
¼ bunch mint leaves
crusty bread, to serve

10 Set the frying pan over a high heat. Start slicing the kingfish finely with a very sharp knife.

9 Finish slicing the kingfish.

8 Arrange the kingfish pieces on a large platter in a single layer. Place the nuts, garlic and olive oil in the frying pan and toss well.

7 Add the breadcrumbs to the frying pan and cook for 30 seconds until just browned.

6 As soon as the breadcrumbs are browned, immediately add the capsicum and tomato to the frying pan and stir well.

5 Stir the spices into the breadcrumb mixture then transfer to a food processor. Pulse several times until it forms a coarse paste. Season lightly with salt and pepper then spread on a large plate to cool. This is the romesco sauce.

4 Chop the lemon into very small pieces. Return the frying pan to the stove and set over a medium heat.

3 Place the mustard seed oil and lemon pieces in the frying pan and cook for 1 minute.

2 Place spoonfuls of romesco sauce on top of the kingfish and then drizzle with fried lemon and the pan oil. Tear the mint leaves.

1 Garnish with torn mint and serve with crusty bread.

MONTE CRISTO WITH ASPARAGUS SALAD

GEAR
chopping board
knife
ribbed griddle
2 medium mixing bowls
vegetable peeler

FOOD
8 slices white bread
4 Tbsp Dijon mustard
200g Gruyère cheese, sliced finely
400g sliced ham off the bone
4 eggs
150ml thickened cream
salt and pepper
cooking oil spray
2 bunches asparagus
½ punnet cherry tomatoes
¼ bunch tarragon
2 Tbsp extra virgin olive oil
1 lemon

10 Set the ribbed griddle over a medium heat. Cut the crusts off the bread and smear one side of each slice with mustard.

9 Divide the Gruyère cheese evenly on top of the mustard.

8 Top half the bread slices with ham, then press together to form four sandwiches.

7 Whisk the eggs and cream together in a medium mixing bowl and season lightly with salt and pepper. Dip each sandwich into the egg mixture.

6 Lightly spray the griddle with cooking oil then lay the sandwiches on the hot surface.

5 Use the vegetable peeler to shave the asparagus spears into long strips, reserving the tips.

4 Cut the cherry tomatoes into quarters. Turn the sandwiches.

3 Pick the tarragon leaves. Combine the tarragon, asparagus and tomatoes in a medium mixing bowl. Dress with olive oil. Cut the lemon in half and drizzle over the salad.

2 Season the salad with salt and pepper then toss well. Remove the sandwiches from the griddle.

1 Cut each sandwich in half and serve with a generous pile of asparagus salad.

PESTO-CHICKEN COLESLAW

GEAR
frying pan
chopping board
knife
large mixing bowl
vegetable peeler
box grater
wooden spoon
small mixing bowl
whisk

FOOD
½ BBQ chicken
¼ cup pine nuts
¼ head green cabbage
1 carrot
2 spring onions
1 vine-ripened tomato
salt and pepper
2 Tbsp pesto
2 Tbsp mayonnaise
¼ bunch basil

10 Set the frying pan over a high heat. Peel the meat off the BBQ chicken.

9 Slice the chicken into fine pieces then place in the large mixing bowl.

8 Pour the pine nuts into the hot frying pan and toss until toasted. Shred the cabbage finely then combine with the chicken.

7 Transfer the pine nuts to the large mixing bowl. Peel the carrot and grate on the coarse blade of the box grater. Add the carrot to the large mixing bowl.

6 Finely slice the spring onion and add to the chicken mixture.

5 Dice the tomato and add to the chicken mixture.

4 Season the salad with salt and pepper, then toss well.

3 Whisk the pesto and mayonnaise together in the small mixing bowl.

2 Stir the mayonnaise dressing through the salad. Pick the basil leaves.

1 Pile the salad on four serving plates and garnish with basil leaves.

Red cabbage works just as well in this recipe.

CRAB AND CASHEW SANG CHOI BAO

GEAR
chopping board
knife
scissors
vegetable peeler
box grater
large mixing bowl
teaspoon
wooden spoon
small mixing bowl

FOOD
1 iceberg lettuce
1 large carrot
2 Lebanese cucumbers
½ bunch mint
½ bunch coriander
1 cup bean shoots
½ cup roasted cashews
2 limes
2 Tbsp dark soy sauce
2 Tbsp sweet chilli sauce
1 tsp sesame oil
200g crab meat
1 long red chilli
2 shallots

10 Carefully separate four large leaves from the lettuce. Use a pair of scissors to trim these leaves, forming perfect cups.

9 Peel the carrot and grate on the coarse blade of a box grater. Transfer carrot to the large mixing bowl.

8 Halve the cucumbers lengthways and remove the seeds with a teaspoon.

7 Slice the cucumbers finely and add to the large mixing bowl.

6 Roughly chop the herbs and add to the large mixing bowl. Mix well.

5 Add the bean shoots and cashews to the large mixing bowl and toss thoroughly. Halve the limes and squeeze their juice into the small mixing bowl. Whisk in the soy, chilli sauce and sesame oil.

4 Pour the dressing over the salad and toss well to combine.

3 Arrange the lettuce cups on individual plates and fill with the salad mixture.

2 Top each lettuce cup with a generous amount of crab meat.

1 Slice the chilli and shallots finely and use to garnish the sang choi bao.

SMOKED TROUT PÂTÉ WITH GARLIC TOASTS

FIRST
turn the sandwich press on

GEAR
chopping board
knife
food processor
mortar and pestle
sandwich press

FOOD
2 smoked trout (approx. 800g in total)
250g cream cheese
1 pickled onion
2 Tbsp extra virgin olive oil
1 bunch dill
salt and pepper
1 loaf Turkish bread
4 cloves garlic
1 bunch thyme
100g unsalted butter
1 tsp dried oregano

10 Peel the skin from the trout and gently remove the fillets ensuring that you do not include any fine bones.

9 Place the trout fillets, cream cheese, pickled onion and olive oil in a food processor and pulse until it forms a coarse paste.

8 Chop the dill finely and add to the food processor. Season lightly with salt and pepper. Pulse several more times to incorporate. Set aside.

7 Slice the Turkish bread in half lengthways. Peel the garlic cloves.

6 Chop the thyme finely and place in the mortar.

5 Add the garlic to the mortar and begin pounding gently to crush the garlic to a smooth paste.

4 Add the butter and oregano to the mortar and pound to form a smooth compound butter. Spread evenly along one half of the Turkish bread. Place the Turkish bread in the sandwich press to grill.

3 Transfer the trout pâté to a serving bowl.

2 Rotate the Turkish bread to ensure even cooking.

1 Cut the Turkish bread into large wedges and place next to the bowl of pâté.

If you don't have a mortar and pestle, crush the garlic with a knife, then combine with the butter and beat with a wooden spoon until smooth.

BABY BEETROOT AND MARINATED FETA TARTLETS WITH WATERCRESS

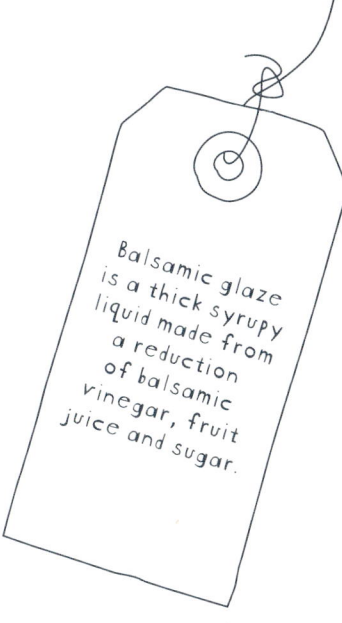

Balsamic glaze is a thick syrupy liquid made from a reduction of balsamic vinegar, fruit juice and sugar.

FIRST
preheat the oven to 180°C

GEAR
pastry brush
4 coffee cups
2 baking trays
chopping board
knife
mixing bowl

FOOD
1 Tbsp chilli oil
4 tortillas
400g can baby beetroots
½ bunch thyme
2 Tbsp extra virgin olive oil
100g pecans
1 red onion
½ bunch watercress
¼ cup pitted Kalamata olives
200g marinated feta cheese
1 Tbsp red wine vinegar
2 tsp balsamic glaze

10 Brush the inside of the coffee cups with chilli oil. Cut the tortillas into 12cm discs then dampen under cold running water.

9 Press the discs into the coffee cups and place on a baking tray. Bake for 8 minutes until golden and crisp. Drain the beetroot then cut them in half.

8 Chop the thyme finely then toss with the beetroots, olive oil and pecans in the mixing bowl. Peel the onion, slice finely and add to the mixture.

7 Transfer the beetroot mixture to a baking tray and roast for 4 minutes until just warmed.

6 Pick the watercress leaves.

5 Halve the olives.

4 Crumble the feta.

3 Combine the beetroot mixture, watercress, olives and feta in the mixing bowl and toss well.

2 Remove the tortilla cups from the oven and arrange on plates. Fill with the beetroot salad mixture.

1 Drizzle with vinegar and balsamic glaze.

DILL CREPES WITH TUNA SALAD

These crepes can be made in batches and frozen for later use. Just make sure you put some freezer plastic or non-stick baking paper between each one.

GEAR
large non-stick frying pan
large mixing bowl
whisk
chopping board
knife
sieve
ladle
small mixing bowl
wooden spoon

FOOD
2 eggs
1 cup milk
1 Tbsp olive oil
½ cup plain flour
½ tsp baking powder
¼ tsp salt
1 bunch dill
cooking oil spray
1 red onion
6 gherkins
1 Tbsp capers
400g can tuna in oil
3 Tbsp mayonnaise
salt and pepper
2 cups baby spinach leaves

10 Set the large non-stick frying pan over a low heat. Break the eggs into the large mixing bowl then whisk in the milk and olive oil.

9 Sift the flour and baking powder together then whisk this and the salt gently into the egg mixture. Chop the dill finely and whisk in.

8 Spray the pan with cooking oil and pour a ladle of crepe batter into the pan. Swirl gently to spread as thinly as possible. Cook gently. Once cooked, set the crepe aside.

7 Peel the onion and dice finely. Dice the gherkins. Chop the capers.

6 Cook a second crepe. Drain the tuna and crumble into the small mixing bowl.

5 Combine the onion, gherkin, capers, tuna and mayonnaise.

4 Cook a third crepe.

3 Season the tuna mixture with salt and pepper.

2 Cook a fourth crepe.

1 Lay spinach leaves down on the crepes and top with tuna mixture. Roll up and cut each crepe in half.

WOK-SEARED BABY OCTOPUS WITH GREEN CURRY AND COCONUT WITH CUCUMBER SALAD

FIRST
set the wok on medium heat

GEAR
wok
mixing bowl
vegetable peeler
chopping board
knife
grater
wooden spoon

FOOD
4 Lebanese cucumbers
2 eschalots
1 red birdseye chilli
1 lime
5cm piece ginger
2 tsp fish sauce
2 tsp soy sauce
¼ tsp caster sugar
1 tsp sesame oil
1 Tbsp peanut oil
800g cleaned baby octopus
2 Tbsp green curry paste
400ml coconut cream
1 bunch coriander
salt and pepper

10 Shave the cucumbers into a mixing bowl with a vegetable peeler, leaving the seed section. Peel the eschalots.

9 Slice the eschalots and chilli very finely with a sharp knife and add to the mixing bowl.

8 Halve the lime and squeeze the juice onto the cucumbers.

7 Grate the ginger into the bowl then add the fish and soy sauces and sugar. Mix well then set aside.

6 Turn the heat under the wok to high and add the sesame and peanut oils.

5 Once the wok is very hot, add the octopus and toss well.

4 Add the green curry paste to the wok and continue cooking, stirring frequently.

3 Add the coconut cream to the wok and stir well. Pick the coriander leaves.

2 Season with salt and pepper and stir in the coriander leaves.

1 Divide the cucumber salad among serving plates and serve the octopus on the side with a generous amount of ginger soy sauce.

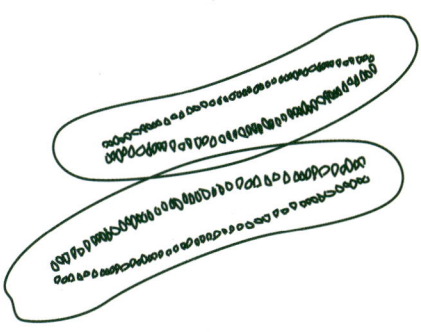

SMALL BITES

BBQ MUSHROOMS WITH FIGS AND BRESAOLA

Bresaola is an Italian air-dried beef, somewhere between prosciutto and jerky, available from good delis. If your local doesn't stock it, replace with shaved sopressa salami.

FIRST
set the ribbed griddle or
  BBQ grill on a medium heat

GEAR
ribbed griddle or BBQ grill
frying pan
chopping board
knife
large mixing bowl
small mixing bowl

FOOD
8 medium Swiss brown
  mushrooms
2 Tbsp avocado oil
½ tsp ground nutmeg
salt and pepper
2 Tbsp dark brown sugar
2 figs
1 eschalot
¼ bunch lemon thyme
120g shaved bresaola
2 Tbsp pepitas
1 tsp balsamic vinegar
2 Tbsp ricotta cheese

10 Place the frying pan over a high heat. Cut the stems off the mushrooms and discard. Place mushroom caps in the large mixing bowl and toss in avocado oil and nutmeg, seasoning with salt and pepper.

9 Place the mushrooms flat-side down on the hot ribbed griddle. Put the brown sugar in the hot frying pan and stir well. Quarter the figs.

8 Once the sugar has caramelised place the fig quarters in the caramel. Peel the eschalot.

7 Finely dice the eschalot and place in the small mixing bowl. Turn the mushrooms. When the figs have softened slightly, remove them from the caramel and set on a plate to cool.

6 Pick the thyme leaves.

5 Tear the bresaola into small pieces and combine with the eschalot. Toss well.

4 Remove the mushrooms from the griddle and set on a plate to cool slightly.

3 Add the pepitas and balsamic vinegar to the bresaola mixture and toss well.

2 Place two mushrooms on each plate together with two fig quarters and top with the bresaola salad.

1 Crumble the ricotta on top of the mushrooms and figs.

SMALL BITES

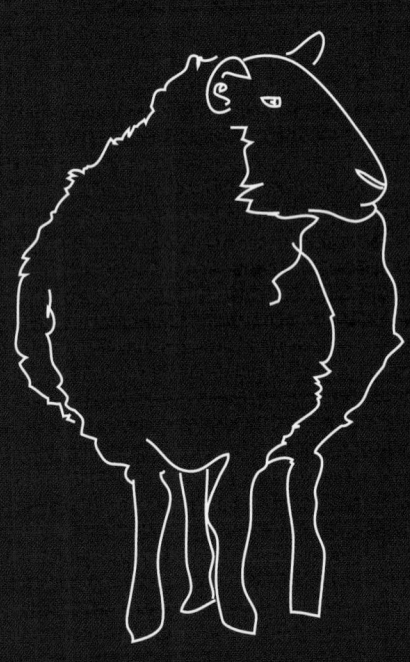

LAMB

KUYBIDEH KABOB, AN IRANIAN STREETFOOD

FIRST
set the ribbed griddle or BBQ grill on medium heat

GEAR
ribbed griddle or BBQ grill
chopping board
knife
large mixing bowl
2 wooden spoons
8 metal skewers
vegetable peeler
box grater
small mixing bowl

FOOD
1 brown onion
2 cloves garlic
½ bunch dill
1kg lamb mince
1 tsp ground turmeric
½ tsp ground cinnamon
¼ tsp ground cardamom
salt and pepper
cooking oil spray
1 Lebanese cucumber
¼ bunch mint
200g natural yoghurt
½ tsp sweet paprika
½ bunch parsley
1 lemon

10 Peel the onion and garlic. Dice both finely.

9 Chop the dill finely and combine with the lamb mince, onion and garlic in the large mixing bowl.

8 Add the spices to the lamb mixture and season generously with salt and pepper. Mix well until very smooth.

7 Form the mince mixture into long cylinders around the metal skewers then spray well with cooking oil. Lay the skewers on the hot ribbed griddle.

6 Peel the cucumber and grate coarsely into the small mixing bowl.

5 Pick the mint leaves and chop finely. Turn the skewers.

4 Combine the mint and yoghurt with the cucumber, season with salt, and mix well.

3 Turn the skewers.

2 Spoon the yoghurt sauce into a ramekin and sprinkle with paprika. Turn the skewers. Chop the parsley very finely. Cut the lemon into quarters.

1 Place two skewers on each plate, sprinkle with chopped parsley, garnish with a lemon quarter and a spoon of sauce.

FRIED LAMB CUTLETS IN WHOLEGRAIN CRUMBS WITH BRUSSELS SPROUTS AND CORN

GEAR
chopping board
knife
5L saucepan
wooden spoon
3 small mixing bowls
whisk
frying pan

FOOD
200ml vegetable oil
8 Brussels sprouts
1 ear corn
2 Tbsp unsalted butter
salt and pepper
3 eggs
½ cup plain flour
1 cup wholegrain breadcrumbs
12 lamb cutlets, French trimmed
4 shallots
1 clove garlic
150ml chicken stock
¼ bunch basil

10 Set the frying pan over a high heat and pour in the vegetable oil. Quarter the Brussels sprouts and cut the kernels off the corn. Put the sprouts, corn and butter in the 5L saucepan and set over a high heat.

9 Break the eggs into a small mixing bowl and whisk well. Place the flour and breadcrumbs in separate small mixing bowls. Coat the cutlets in flour, then dip in egg. Stir the corn mixture.

8 Coat the lamb generously in breadcrumbs then arrange in the frying pan. Stir the corn mixture.

7 Slice the shallots finely and add to the saucepan. Stir well.

6 Season the corn mixture with salt and pepper and mix. Peel the garlic and slice finely.

5 Turn the cutlets. Add the chicken stock to the saucepan.

4 Stir the corn mixture. Pick the basil leaves.

3 Add the garlic to the saucepan and adjust seasoning.

2 Remove the cutlets from the frying pan and drain on absorbent paper.

1 Stir the basil into the corn mixture and divide among four plates, then arrange cutlets on top.

'French trimming' is a butcher's technique that cleans up the cutlet bones so they present really well.

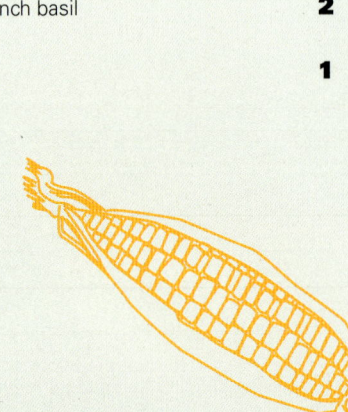

LAMB BACKSTRAP STUFFED WITH BLUE CHEESE ON CREAMY TOMATO LENTILS

GEAR

large frying pan
5L saucepan
chopping board
knife
8 metal skewers
pastry brush
wooden spoon
colander

FOOD

4 x 200g lamb backstraps (eye of loin)
120g strong blue cheese
salt and pepper
1 Tbsp vegetable oil
1 eschalot
1 clove garlic
1 Tbsp extra virgin olive oil
2 vine-ripened tomatoes
1 bay leaf
1 chicken stock cube
300ml cream
400g can brown lentils
½ bunch marjoram

10 Set the large frying pan over a high heat. Set the 5L saucepan over a medium heat. Use a sharp knife to make a lateral incision in each backstrap, leaving the ends intact. Cut the cheese into eight slices.

9 Stuff 2 slices of cheese into each backstrap and secure each open side with a metal skewer. Season with salt and pepper then brush with vegetable oil.

8 Place the backstraps into the hot frying pan. Peel the eschalot and garlic and chop both finely, then transfer to the saucepan with the olive oil and stir well.

7 Dice the tomatoes. Stir the eschalot mixture.

6 Add the tomato, bay leaf and stock cube to the saucepan and stir well.

5 Turn the backstraps. Pour the cream into the saucepan, turn the heat to high and stir thoroughly.

4 Season the tomato mixture with salt and pepper. Drain the can of lentils in a colander then rinse well under running water.

3 Add the lentils to the saucepan and mix. Pick the marjoram leaves.

2 Remove the backstraps from the frying pan. Stir the marjoram leaves into the creamy lentils then divide among four plates.

1 Pull out the skewers from the backstraps, then carve and arrange on top.

BUTTERFLIED LAMB NECK FILLET WITH CHEESY FRIED CAULIFLOWER

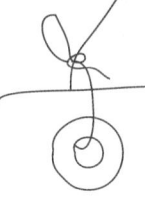

Marsala is a sweet style of fortified wine from the town of Marsala in Sicily. Its distinctly dark colour and oaky smell are superbly matched with meats and mushrooms.

FIRST
set the ribbed griddle or BBQ grill on high heat

GEAR
ribbed griddle or BBQ grill
large frying pan
chopping board
knife
1L saucepan
wooden spoon
box grater

FOOD
4 x 200g boneless lamb neck fillets
1 Tbsp avocado oil
salt and pepper
½ head cauliflower
2 Tbsp extra virgin olive oil
4 cloves garlic
¼ bunch thyme
¼ bunch sage
1 lemon
½ tsp ground cumin
1 Tbsp Marsala wine
½ cup fresh breadcrumbs
60g Parmesan cheese
¼ bunch mint
1 Tbsp balsamic vinegar

10 Set the large frying pan over a medium heat. Use a sharp knife to slice down the centre of the neck fillets cutting three-quarters of the way through. Open the fillets up flat (butterflying).

9 Rub the lamb with avocado oil, salt and pepper and place on the hot ribbed griddle or BBQ grill. Use a sharp knife to remove the florets from the cauliflower.

8 Place the cauliflower and olive oil in the hot frying pan and toss well. Peel the garlic and slice into fine pieces.

7 Toss the cauliflower. Chop the thyme and sage. Cut the lemon into quarters and set aside.

6 Add the thyme, sage, garlic and cumin to the cauliflower and toss well.

5 Turn the lamb. Add the Marsala to the frying pan and mix thoroughly. Add the breadcrumbs and stir.

4 Grate the Parmesan finely. Stir the cauliflower and remove from the heat. Pick the mint leaves.

3 Stir the Parmesan into the cauliflower and season with salt and a generous amount of black pepper. Drizzle the lamb with balsamic vinegar.

2 Remove the lamb from the ribbed griddle and carve. Stir the mint leaves into the cauliflower and divide among serving plates.

1 Arrange the lamb on top and garnish with lemon wedges.

LAMB 'BIT-OVER-A-MINUTE' STEAK WITH MINT SPÄTZLE AND PEAS

FIRST
boil 3L water in kettle

GEAR
ribbed griddle plate or BBQ grill
5L saucepan
3L saucepan
chopping board
knife
meat mallet
2 large mixing bowls
whisk
colander
spatula
slotted spoon
small mixing bowl

FOOD
3L boiling water
1L chicken stock
2 x 240g lamb rumps
2 tsp hot paprika
salt and pepper
1 egg
½ cup milk
½ bunch mint
½ cup plain flour
2 Tbsp extra virgin olive oil
200g peas
cooking oil spray
1 Tbsp unsalted butter
1 lemon

10 Set the ribbed griddle over a medium heat. Set the 5L saucepan over a high heat and fill with the boiling water. Set the 3L saucepan over a medium heat and pour in the chicken stock. Slice the lamb rumps in half.

9 Hammer the lamb rump steaks with a meat mallet between sheets of freezer plastic until 1cm thick then sprinkle with paprika, salt and pepper and set aside.

8 Break the egg into a large mixing bowl, pour in the milk and whisk well. Finely chop the mint and stir into the egg mixture.

7 Slowly add the flour to the egg mixture, stirring gently. Season generously with salt and pepper.

6 Set the colander over the 5L saucepan of simmering water. Pour the batter into the colander and press through with a spatula. Turn the heat under the ribbed griddle to high.

5 As soon as the small dumplings, or spätzle, float on the surface scoop them out with a slotted spoon and transfer to the second large mixing bowl. Toss in olive oil.

4 Plunge the peas into the simmering chicken stock and cook for 2 minutes until tender. Spray the lamb steaks with cooking oil.

3 Place the steaks on the hot ribbed riddle. Spoon the butter into the small mixing bowl. Halve the lemon and squeeze the juice onto the butter.

2 Turn the steaks. Divide the spätzle among serving plates. Scoop the peas out of the stock with a slotted spoon and toss in the butter and lemon juice. Season lightly. Spoon the spätzle around.

1 Top each serve with a lamb steak.

LAMB

LAMB AND PANCETTA SKEWERS WITH GREEN BEAN AND TOMATO SAUTÉ

GEAR
2 frying pans
chopping boards
knife
4 metal skewers
tongs

FOOD
16 fine slices flat pancetta
16 pieces diced lamb (600g)
½ loaf sourdough bread
2 Tbsp unsalted butter
1 cup green beans
1 Tbsp chilli oil
1 clove garlic
2 punnets cherry tomatoes
½ bunch sage
½ cup breadcrumbs
salt and pepper

10 Set the two frying pans over a medium heat. Lay the pancetta slices out on a chopping board.

9 Place a cube of lamb on one end of each piece of pancetta and roll up.

8 Cut the bread into 12 cubes each approximately the same size as the lamb.

7 Skewer 4 pieces of lamb onto each skewer, alternating with pieces of bread. Spoon the butter into one frying pan and arrange the skewers in the hot pan.

6 Roughly chop the beans then place into the second frying pan with the chilli oil. Stir well.

5 Turn the skewers. Peel the garlic and slice finely.

4 Add the garlic to the green beans and stir well. Add the tomatoes.

3 Pick the sage leaves and add to the tomato mixture, then stir in the breadcrumbs. Season well with salt and pepper.

2 Season the skewers with pepper only, then remove from the frying pan.

1 Divide the tomato mixture among serving plates, then top each one with a skewer.

Pancetta is a cured pork smallgood, much like prosciutto. But whereas prosciutto is made from pork leg, pancetta is made from the belly. It comes in a flat and a round style. The flat works much better in this dish.

CHARGRILLED LAMB CUTLETS WITH PARSLEY SALSA AND SAVOURY FRENCH TOAST

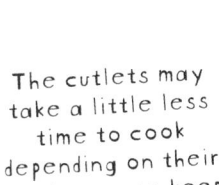

The cutlets may take a little less time to cook depending on their thickness, so keep an eye on them.

GEAR
ribbed griddle or BBQ grill
chopping board
knife
tongs
3 large mixing bowls
wooden spoon
frying pan
whisk
egg slice

FOOD
12 lamb cutlets, French trimmed
2 Tbsp extra virgin olive oil
½ tsp ground allspice
salt and pepper
2 bunches flat-leaf parsley
2 lemons
2 cloves garlic
1 small green chilli
¼ cup pitted Kalamata olives
4 eggs
150ml double cream
1 Tbsp Dijon mustard
1 Tbsp tomato paste
4 slices thick-cut sourdough bread
2 Tbsp unsalted butter

10 Set a ribbed griddle over a high heat. Toss the lamb cutlets in olive oil and allspice in a large mixing bowl. Season generously with salt and pepper. Set aside.

9 Finely chop the parsley and place in another large mixing bowl.

8 Grate the lemon zest onto the parsley. Peel the garlic and mince it, then add to the parsley mixture.

7 Slice the chilli finely. Chop the olives finely. Add both to the parsley mixture then toss thoroughly. Set the frying pan over a medium heat.

6 Arrange the cutlets on the hot ribbed griddle. Break the eggs into the third mixing bowl then pour in the cream, mustard and tomato paste. Season with salt and pepper then whisk well.

5 Dip the bread slices into the egg mixture and coat well to ensure that the bread absorbs as much of this mixture as possible.

4 Turn the cutlets. Put the butter into the frying pan and add the soaked bread slices.

3 Season the parsley salsa lightly with salt and pepper. Turn the French toast.

2 Halve the lemons and squeeze their juice over the lamb cutlets, cook for another 30 seconds, then remove from the griddle. Remove the French toast from the frying pan.

1 Set a slice of French toast on each plate and top with three cutlets and a generous spoon of parsley salsa.

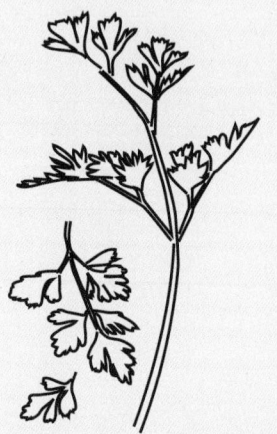

SHIRAZ-BASTED LAMB BACKSTRAP WITH CHICKPEAS AND SPINACH

Choose a Shiraz without too much tannin for a smoother result.

GEAR
3L saucepan
large frying pan
5L saucepan
colander
chopping board
knife
pastry brush

FOOD
250ml Shiraz
2 Tbsp golden syrup
1 Tbsp extra virgin olive oil
4 x 200g lamb backstraps
salt and pepper
400g can chickpeas
1 red onion
1 Tbsp mustard seed oil
2 bunches English spinach
1 chicken stock cube
100ml sherry
1 tsp unsalted butter

10 Pour the Shiraz and golden syrup into the 3L saucepan and set over a high heat. Pour the olive oil into the large frying pan and set over a high heat. Set the 5L saucepan over a medium heat.

9 Season the lamb backstraps with salt and pepper. Drain the chickpeas and rinse in a colander under running water. Peel the onion.

8 Place the backstraps in the hot frying pan. Finely dice the onion and add to the 5L saucepan with the mustard seed oil. Stir well.

7 Stir the onions well.

6 Once the Shiraz has reduced by three-quarters remove from the heat. Turn the backstraps.

5 Add the chickpeas to the onions and stir well. Pick the spinach leaves and rinse in a colander under running water.

4 Add the spinach, stock cube, sherry and butter to the 5L saucepan and season with salt and pepper. Turn the backstraps.

3 Baste the backstraps with the Shiraz mixture and turn. Baste again.

2 Turn the backstraps and baste again. Divide the chickpea mixture among serving plates.

1 Carve the backstraps and arrange over the chickpeas and spinach.

BERBER-SPICED LAMB CUTLETS WITH CLASSIC WALDORF SALAD

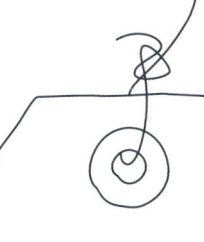

Berber spice blend is the traditional flavour of Ethiopian food. If you can find ajowan seeds from a good spice dealer, use them in place of cumin. If not, the cumin will do just fine.

FIRST
set the ribbed griddle or BBQ grill on high heat

GEAR
ribbed griddle or BBQ grill
frying pan
chopping board
knife
2 large mixing bowls
wooden spoon
tongs

FOOD
12 lamb cutlets, French trimmed
salt and pepper
1 tsp ground cumin
½ tsp ground fenugreek
¼ tsp ground cardamom
¼ tsp ground cloves
½ tsp ground coriander
½ tsp ground cinnamon
¼ tsp ground ginger
¼ tsp ground chilli
2 Tbsp mustard seed oil
2 sweet red apples (Braeburn, Fuji, Pink Lady)
4 sticks celery
½ cup walnuts
¼ cup raisins
¼ cup mayonnaise

10 Season the lamb cutlets with salt and a generous amount of black pepper.

9 Set the frying pan over a medium heat then add the spices. Cook, stirring constantly, until the spices become aromatic. Transfer to a large mixing bowl.

8 Stir the mustard seed oil into the spices and rub mixture onto the cutlets.

7 Arrange the cutlets on the hot ribbed griddle.

6 Remove the cheeks from the apples, then cut into very fine slices. Place in the other large mixing bowl.

5 Slice the celery very finely and add to apple slices.

4 Turn the cutlets. Crush the walnuts roughly and add to the apple mixture.

3 Add the raisins and mayonnaise to the apple mixture and mix thoroughly.

2 Season the waldorf salad lightly then divide among serving plates.

1 Remove the cutlets from the ribbed griddle and arrange next to the salad.

GRILLED CHUMP CHOPS WITH EGGPLANT VINDALOO

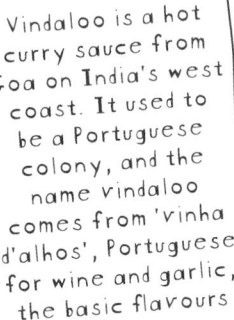

Vindaloo is a hot curry sauce from Goa on India's west coast. It used to be a Portuguese colony, and the name vindaloo comes from 'vinha d'alhos', Portuguese for wine and garlic, the basic flavours of the sauce.

FIRST
set the ribbed griddle or BBQ grill on medium heat

GEAR
ribbed griddle or BBQ grill
5L saucepan
large mixing bowl
chopping board
knife
wooden spoon

FOOD
8 centre-cut lamb chump chops (1.2kg)
2 Tbsp mustard seed oil
salt and pepper
1 brown onion
2 Tbsp peanut oil
1 large eggplant
1 green capsicum
6 fresh curry leaves
1 cinnamon stick
1 Tbsp black mustard seeds
2 Tbsp vindaloo paste
1 cup chicken stock
1 lime
½ bunch coriander
4 Tbsp natural yoghurt

10 Set the 5L saucepan over a high heat. Toss the chops in mustard seed oil in a large mixing bowl and season with salt and pepper. Peel the onion and slice very finely, then place in the saucepan along with the peanut oil.

9 Dice the eggplant and capsicum into 2cm cubes, and add to the saucepan. Add the curry leaves, cinnamon stick and mustard seeds and stir well.

8 Arrange the chops on the hot ribbed griddle. Season the eggplant mixture.

7 Stir the vindaloo paste into the eggplant mixture.

6 Add half the chicken stock to the eggplant mixture and stir well.

5 Add the remaining chicken stock to the eggplant mixture and stir well. Cut the lime in half.

4 Turn the chops.

3 Squeeze the lime juice over the chops.

2 Divide the eggplant vindaloo among serving plates. Pick the coriander leaves.

1 Arrange the chops on the eggplant vindaloo then garnish with yoghurt and coriander leaves.

LAMB

SOY-GLAZED LAMB FILLETS WITH TREACLE ON CRUSHED WHITE BEANS

FIRST
boil 1L water in kettle

GEAR
two 3L saucepans
chopping board
knife
frying pan
pastry brush
colander
food processor
large mixing bowl
wooden spoon
slotted spoon

FOOD
1 lime
¼ cup Japanese soy sauce
¼ cup treacle
1L boiling water
1 tsp white wine vinegar
salt and pepper
2 eggs
2 x 400g cans white beans
1 Tbsp vegetable oil
8 lamb fillets (800g)
¼ bunch rosemary
¼ cup extra virgin olive oil
2 lemons

10 Halve the lime and squeeze the juice into a 3L saucepan. Add the soy sauce and treacle then set the saucepan over a high heat. Set the frying pan over a high heat.

9 Pour the boiling water into the other 3L saucepan and add the white wine vinegar. Season lightly with salt. Turn the heat to low and gently break in the eggs.

8 Drain the white beans in the colander then rinse well under running water.

7 Add the vegetable oil to the hot frying pan and add the lamb fillets.

6 Once the soy mixture has thickened remove from the heat. Turn the lamb fillets.

5 When the eggs are soft-poached, remove from the simmering water with a slotted spoon and place in the large mixing bowl. Place the white beans in a food processor and pulse several times until coarsely crushed. Don't overmix. Turn the lamb fillets and reduce the heat to medium.

4 Transfer the white beans to the large mixing bowl and mix with the eggs. Pick the rosemary leaves and add to the bowl. Turn the lamb fillets.

3 Pour the olive oil over the beans. Halve the lemons and squeeze in the juice. Season with salt and pepper, then mix well. Baste the lamb fillets with the soy mixture and turn.

2 Baste the lamb fillets and turn again. Divide the bean mixture among serving plates.

1 Arrange the lamb fillets over the beans and drizzle with some pan juices.

TANDOORI 'LAMB-BURGER' WITH AVOCADO AND HUMMOUS

FIRST
turn the sandwich press on

GEAR
sandwich press
large frying pan
chopping board
knife
large mixing bowl
wooden spoon

FOOD
½ bunch coriander
600g lamb mince
3 Tbsp tikka masala paste
2 tsp onion powder
2 eggs
½ cup breadcrumbs
salt and pepper
2 Tbsp mustard seed oil
1 loaf Turkish bread
2 avocados
2 tomatoes
4 Tbsp hummous
8 slices Swiss cheese
¼ bunch basil leaves
1 cup rocket leaves

10 Set the large frying pan over a medium heat. Finely chop the coriander and transfer to the large mixing bowl.

9 Add the lamb mince, tikka masala paste, onion powder, eggs and breadcrumbs to the large mixing bowl, season with salt and pepper, and mix well.

8 Form eight balls from the mince mixture, then flatten to form 1cm-thick discs. Pour the mustard seed oil into the frying pan and arrange the patties on top.

7 Cut the Turkish bread in half lengthways and then into four sections, then toast in the sandwich press.

6 Cut the avocados in half, remove the seeds, scoop out the flesh and slice into a fan.

5 Slice the tomatoes into 1cm-thick pieces. Turn the patties.

4 Remove the bread from the sandwich press and lay on the chopping board. Smear pieces of bread with hummous. Place a slice of tomato on each piece of bread.

3 Place a lamb patty on each burger and place back in the sandwich press.

2 Pick the basil leaves.

1 Remove the burgers from the sandwich press. Open and place slices of cheese on top of each one and finish with avocado slices, basil and rocket.

BEEF

A PIE OF SORTS: CHUNKY BEEF IN TOMATO WITH CRISPY FILO WAFERS

FIRST
turn the oven on to 220°C

GEAR
frying pan
chopping board
knife
baking tray
tongs
wooden spoon

FOOD
4 sheets filo pastry
2 Tbsp avocado oil
1 Tbsp poppy seeds
600g beef fillet
2 Tbsp extra virgin olive oil
1 brown onion
2 cloves garlic
salt and pepper
1 tsp dried Italian herbs
2 x 400g cans crushed tomatoes
2 Tbsp BBQ sauce
½ bunch flat-leaf parsley

10 Set the large frying pan over a medium heat. Brush the filo sheets with avocado oil, then sprinkle with poppy seeds and lay in a stack. Cut filo stack into four pieces, then lay on a lined baking tray and place in the oven.

9 Dice the beef fillet into 1cm cubes. Pour the olive oil into the hot frying pan. Peel the onion and garlic.

8 Place the beef in the hot frying pan and toss well. Slice the onion and garlic finely.

7 Add the onion and garlic to the frying pan, season with salt and pepper, and stir well.

6 Stir the Italian herbs into the beef mixture.

5 Add the tomatoes to the beef mixture and turn the heat to high.

4 Stir the BBQ sauce into the beef mixture. Chop the parsley finely.

3 Stir the parsley into the beef mixture.

2 Check the seasoning and adjust as necessary.

1 Remove the filo sheets from the oven. Spoon the beef mixture into gratin dishes and top with crisp filo wafers.

'BISTECCA ALLA FIORENTINA': TUSCAN T-BONE WITH LEMON, OLIVE OIL AND PARSLEY

FIRST
set the ribbed griddle or BBQ grill on high heat

GEAR
ribbed griddle or BBQ grill
pastry brush
mortar and pestle
chopping board
knife
steamer
large mixing bowl
tongs

FOOD
4 x 300g T-bone steaks
2 Tbsp extra virgin olive oil
salt and pepper
2 lemons
½ bunch thyme
1 bunch parsley
4 bunches broccolini
2 Tbsp sliced almonds
1 Tbsp unsalted butter

10 Brush the T-bones with olive oil and season with a generous amount of black pepper. Fill the steamer with hot water and set over a high heat.

9 Place the T-bones on the hot ribbed griddle.

8 Zest the lemons and roughly chop the thyme then place both in the mortar. Add 2 Tbsp salt and pound well until smooth.

7 Season the top side of the steaks with the lemon-herb salt.

6 Chop the parsley finely. Cut the cheeks off both lemons and remove the seeds.

5 Turn the steaks. Cut the broccolini into 5cm lengths.

4 Sprinkle the top side of the steak with the lemon-herb salt. Place the broccolini pieces in the steamer.

3 Put the almonds and butter in the large mixing bowl.

2 Add the broccolini to the mixing bowl and season with salt and pepper. Divide among serving plates.

1 Place a steak on each plate and garnish with chopped parsley and a lemon cheek.

BEEF

BEEF AND ASPARAGUS ROTOLI WITH GRILLED RADICCHIO

FIRST
set the ribbed griddle or BBQ grill on medium heat

GEAR
ribbed griddle or BBQ grill
chopping board
knife
tongs
toothpicks
pastry brush
small mixing bowl

FOOD
600g beef rump
120g provolone cheese
16 spears asparagus
2 Tbsp extra virgin olive oil
salt and pepper
2 heads radicchio
2 Tbsp avocado oil
1 bunch oregano
1 Tbsp pine nuts
1 orange
1 Tbsp honey

10 Slice the beef rump into eight thin slices. Cut the provolone into eight slices.

9 Beat the beef pieces with a meat mallet to flatten and tenderise, then lay them on the chopping board. Trim the asparagus spears.

8 Place two asparagus spears and a piece of provolone on each piece of beef and roll up.

7 Secure the rotoli with toothpicks then coat with olive oil and season with salt and pepper. Place on the hot ribbed griddle.

6 Strip the outer leaves from the heads of radicchio leaving the stems intact, then cut in half.

5 Drizzle the radicchio halves with avocado oil and season with salt and pepper. Place on the ribbed griddle.

4 Turn the rotoli. Chop the oregano and pine nuts finely and transfer to the small mixing bowl.

3 Turn the radicchio. Zest the orange into the small mixing bowl. Cut the orange in half and squeeze the juice into the small mixing bowl. Stir in the honey. Season with salt and pepper.

2 Remove the rotoli from the ribbed griddle.

1 Place a radicchio half on each of four plates, then top with the oregano and pine nut mixture. Arrange two rotoli on each plate.

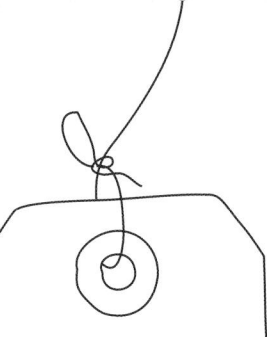

Provolone is a semi-hard cows' milk cheese that comes from the Po valley in northern Italy. Its distinct sweet-sour flavour and good melting properties make it ideal for combining with meats.

EGYPTIAN BEEF KOFTE

FIRST
set the ribbed griddle or BBQ grill on high heat

GEAR
ribbed griddle or BBQ grill
3L saucepan
chopping board
knife
large mixing bowl
4 metal skewers
stick blender

FOOD
1 cup chicken stock
1 dried red chilli
¼ tsp ground nutmeg
1 onion
½ bunch coriander
2 slices soft bread
800g beef mince
2 tsp ground allspice
1 tsp ground cinnamon
1 tsp cracked black pepper
2 Tbsp milk
1 egg
salt and pepper
1 Tbsp extra virgin olive oil
½ cup canned apricot halves in light syrup
1 lemon

10 Place the chicken stock, dried chilli and nutmeg in the 3L saucepan and set over a medium heat. Peel the onion.

9 Chop the coriander roughly. Tear the bread into small pieces.

8 Dice the onion very finely then transfer to the large mixing bowl. Add the beef, spices, coriander, bread, milk and egg, season with salt and pepper, then mix thoroughly.

7 Form the beef mixture into 16 x 4cm balls, then pierce on four metal skewers. Drizzle with olive oil and place on the hot ribbed griddle.

6 Add the apricots to the chicken stock mixture.

5 Turn the kofte.

4 Halve the lemon.

3 Squeeze the lemon juice over the kofte.

2 Puree the apricot mixture with a stick blender. Remove the kofte from the ribbed griddle.

1 Spoon some apricot sauce onto each serving plate, then arrange the kofte on top.

PEPPERED NEW YORK STRIPLOIN STEAK WITH SPICY TOMATO BUTTER AND PEAS

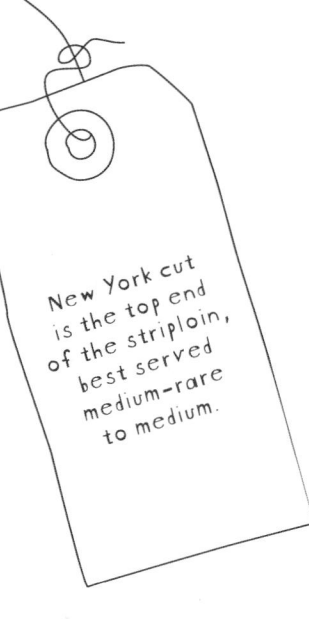

New York cut is the top end of the striploin, best served medium-rare to medium.

FIRST
set the ribbed griddle or BBQ grill on medium heat

GEAR
ribbed griddle or BBQ grill
3L saucepan
chopping board
knife
food processor
tongs

FOOD
500ml chicken stock
4 x 220g New York striploin steaks
1 tsp fine salt
3 Tbsp cracked black pepper
1 Tbsp vegetable oil
2 eschalots
150g soft unsalted butter
2 Tbsp tomato paste
1 tsp Tabasco sauce
2 tsp Worcestershire sauce
½ tsp ground nutmeg
¼ tsp ground cloves
2 cups peas
½ bunch flat-leaf parsley
salt and pepper
2 Tbsp extra virgin olive oil

10 Set the 3L saucepan over a medium heat and pour in the chicken stock. Sprinkle the steaks with salt and then press well with cracked pepper. Drizzle with vegetable oil.

9 Place the steaks on the hot ribbed griddle.

8 Peel the eschalots and dice finely.

7 Place the eschalots in the food processor and pulse several times. Add the butter and tomato paste and pulse several more times.

6 Add the Tabasco, Worcestershire and spices into the food processor and pulse several times.

5 Turn the steaks.

4 Add the peas to the simmering chicken stock. Chop the parsley.

3 Season the butter mixture with salt and pepper.

2 Drain the peas and toss with the olive oil and parsley. Remove the steaks from the ribbed griddle.

1 Carve the steaks and garnish with peas. Spoon some flavoured butter over the steak.

SKIRT STEAK WITH SALTED APPLES AND DUKKAH

FIRST
set the ribbed griddle or BBQ grill on high heat

GEAR
ribbed griddle or BBQ grill
mortar and pestle
hand grater
tongs
chopping board
knife
apple corer
mandoline slicer
medium mixing bowl

FOOD
800g good-quality skirt steak (marble score 5+)
salt and pepper
1 Tbsp avocado oil
1 tsp cumin seeds
¼ tsp caraway seeds
1 tsp white peppercorns
1 lime
2 tsp salt flakes
4 sweet apples (Braeburn, Fuji, Pink Lady)
¼ bunch watercress
1 tsp tarragon vinegar
1 Tbsp extra virgin olive oil
2 Tbsp pistachio dukkah

10 Season the steak generously with salt and pepper, then drizzle with avocado oil. Set aside.

9 Place the cumin, caraway and peppercorns in the mortar, then grate the lime zest in as well. Add the salt flakes and begin to pound.

8 Pound the spiced salt until it forms a smooth mixture.

7 Place the skirt steak on the hot ribbed griddle. Core the apples.

6 Shave the apples into very fine slices using the mandoline slicer, then transfer to the medium mixing bowl.

5 Turn the skirt steak. Dust the apple slices with spice salt and toss well.

4 Pick the watercress leaves into sprigs and divide into four bunches.

3 Drizzle the apples with tarragon vinegar and olive oil. Toss well.

2 Remove the steak from the ribbed griddle. Make a stack of apple slices on each serving plate. Place a watercress bunch alongside.

1 Carve the steaks and arrange next to the apples, then drizzle with remaining salad dressing. Sprinkle the dukkah over the steak.

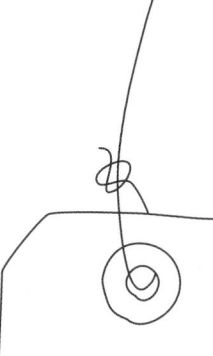

Skirt steak can be tricky. Choose a good, well-marbled piece and cook it no more than medium: the results are amazing. Too lean or overcook it and it's too tough.

MASSAMAN-FLAVOURED TOURNEDOS WITH LENTILS, YOGHURT AND CURRANTS

GEAR
2 frying pans
large mixing bowl
chopping board
knife
wooden spoon
colander
5L saucepan
tongs

FOOD
4 x 180g tenderloin fillets
salt and pepper
1 Tbsp Massaman curry paste
1 Tbsp peanut oil
400g can brown lentils
1 chicken stock cube
1 tsp garam masala
1 tsp cornflour
250ml liquid beef stock
1 long red chilli
1 zucchini
¼ cup currants
½ bunch mint
¼ bunch coriander
¼ cup natural yoghurt

10 Set the two frying pans over a high heat. Slice each tenderloin fillet into three medallions and place in the large mixing bowl. Season with salt and pepper, top with the Massaman curry paste and peanut oil, then mix well.

9 Drain the lentils in a colander and rinse well under cold running water. Place the lentils in the 5L saucepan along with the stock cube and garam masala. Set over a high heat.

8 Mix the cornflour and beef stock and add to the lentil mixture. Cut the chilli into fine slices and add to the saucepan.

7 Dice the zucchini finely. Add the zucchini and currants to the lentils.

6 Place the beef pieces in the frying pans.

5 Pick the mint and coriander leaves.

4 Turn the beef pieces.

3 Season the lentil mixture.

2 Remove the beef pieces from the frying pans.

1 Stir the herbs into the lentil mixture then arrange the tournedos on top. Garnish with yoghurt.

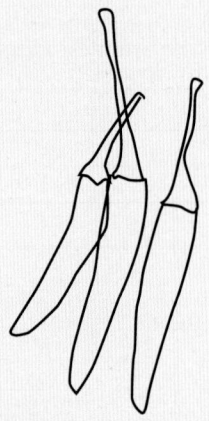

HIGH-SPEED STROGANOFF

FIRST
boil 500ml water in kettle

GEAR
5L saucepan
large mixing bowl
wooden spoon
chopping board
knife
box grater

FOOD
600g beef strips
1 Tbsp flour
1 tsp caraway seeds
2 Tbsp unsalted butter
2 brown onions
2 cloves garlic
200g button mushrooms
3 large washed potatoes
1 chicken stock cube
½ cup brandy
500ml boiling water
150ml double cream
2 tsp mustard
salt and pepper
¼ bunch dill
1 tsp sweet paprika
¼ cup sour cream

10 Set the 5L saucepan over a high heat. Toss the beef strips with the flour in the large mixing bowl. Add beef strips to the saucepan with the caraway seeds and butter. Stir well.

9 Peel the onions and slice finely, then add to the saucepan. Stir thoroughly.

8 Peel the garlic and mince finely, then stir into the beef mixture.

7 Roughly chop the mushrooms and add to the saucepan, then stir in.

6 Grate the potatoes coarsely, squeeze out the excess water, and stir into the saucepan. Crumble the chicken stock cube into the mixture.

5 Pour the brandy into the saucepan, stir well, and cook for 30 seconds. Pour in the boiling water and cream.

4 Stir the mustard into the stroganoff and season well.

3 Pick the dill sprigs.

2 Stir well.

1 Adjust the seasoning as needed, then serve the stroganoff garnished with dill, paprika and sour cream.

Traditionally beef stroganoff is served with rice, but this express version uses grated potato as the primary starch.

CORNED BEEF HASH
WITH GRILLED GOATS' CHEESE

Hash is a traditional dish from Louisiana that gets its name from the French speakers who originally lived there. 'Hacher' is French for 'to chop', and refers to the fact that all the ingredients are chopped down before cooking.

FIRST
set the grill on medium heat

GEAR
wok
vegetable peeler
box grater
chopping board
knife
wooden spoon

FOOD
1 turnip
1 large potato
1 carrot
2 Tbsp vegetable oil
1 stick celery
400g thick-sliced corned beef
2 tsp mustard powder
2 cloves garlic
2 tsp dried thyme
250ml liquid beef stock
1 baguette
2 Tbsp extra virgin olive oil
salt and pepper
4 shallots
120g goats' cheese

10 Set the wok on a high heat. Peel the turnip, potato and carrot, then shred coarsely on a box grater.

9 Add the vegetable oil to the wok then stir in the grated vegetables. Cut the celery into fine slices and mix in.

8 Slice the corned beef into large strips.

7 Stir the beef into the vegetable mixture. Sprinkle with mustard powder. Peel the garlic and chop finely.

6 Stir in the garlic and dried thyme.

5 Add the beef stock to the wok and stir thoroughly. Cut the baguette into eight thick slices and drizzle with olive oil. Season the bread with salt and pepper.

4 Place the bread slices under the grill. Slice the shallots finely.

3 Stir the hash and season with salt and pepper.

2 Turn the bread slices and smear the un-toasted side with goats' cheese. Place back under the grill, cheese-side up.

1 Stir the shallots into the hash and divide among serving plates. Garnish with cheese toasts.

NEAPOLITAN VEAL CHOPS

FIRST
turn on the grill
set the frying pan on high heat

GEAR
frying pan
3L saucepan
chopping board
knife
tongs
large mixing bowl

FOOD
4 x 230g veal chops
salt and pepper
2 Tbsp extra virgin olive oil
4 pickled onions
2 tsp capers
¼ cup black olives
½ cup red wine
500ml chunky tomato sauce
1 tsp brown sugar
1 bunch oregano
2 bunches rocket
1 Tbsp avocado oil
2 tsp red wine vinegar
12 pieces bocconcini cheese

10 Season the veal chops with salt and pepper then drizzle with olive oil. Place the chops in the hot frying pan. Set the 3L saucepan on a medium heat.

9 Chop the pickled onions finely.

8 Chop the capers and olives, then add to the saucepan with the onion, wine and chunky tomato sauce.

7 Turn the veal chops.

6 Mix the brown sugar into the tomato sauce. Pick the oregano leaves.

5 Season the tomato sauce with salt and pepper.

4 Turn the veal chops and pour the tomato sauce into the frying pan. Turn the heat to medium.

3 Dress the rocket with avocado oil and vinegar in the large mixing bowl, then season lightly with salt and pepper. Place the bocconcini on top of the veal chops and set under the grill.

2 Divide the salad among serving plates.

1 Place a veal chop next to each pile of salad, then top with sauce. Garnish with oregano leaves.

SCOTCH FILLET WITH SALSA VERDE AND CAVALO NERO

FIRST
set the ribbed griddle or BBQ grill on medium heat

GEAR
ribbed griddle or BBQ grill
chopping board
knife
tongs
mortar and pestle
large frying pan

FOOD
4 x 220g scotch fillet steaks
salt and pepper
1 Tbsp mustard seed oil
1 bunch flat-leaf parsley
½ bunch thyme
¼ bunch mint
2 cloves garlic
2 tsp capers
2 anchovy fillets
1 tsp white wine vinegar
½ cup extra virgin olive oil
2 bunches cavalo nero
2 Tbsp avocado oil
2 lemons

10 Season steaks with salt and pepper, then drizzle with mustard seed oil. Pick the parsley leaves. Peel the garlic.

9 Place the steaks on the ribbed griddle. Pick the thyme and mint leaves.

8 Place the garlic, capers and anchovies in the mortar and pound until smooth. Set the large frying pan over a medium heat.

7 Add half the herbs to the mortar and continue pounding.

6 Add the remaining herbs to the mortar and continue pounding.

5 Turn the steaks. Stir the vinegar and olive oil into the salsa verde, then season with salt and pepper.

4 Place the cavalo nero and avocado oil in the hot frying pan and toss well.

3 Cut the lemons in half and squeeze the juice into the frying pan, then season with salt and a generous amount of pepper. Remove from the heat.

2 Remove the steaks from the heat. Divide the cavalo nero among serving plates.

1 Carve the steaks and arrange on the cavalo nero. Garnish with salsa verde.

Cavalo nero is Italian black cabbage, a tough green leafy vegetable available throughout the colder months of the year. It looks a little like dark curly silverbeet.

IRISH STEAK AND EGGS

FIRST
set the frying pan on high heat

GEAR
large frying pan
3L saucepan
chopping board
knife
tongs
slotted spoon

FOOD
4 x 220g sirloin steaks
salt and pepper
1 Tbsp vegetable oil
800ml stout
1 Tbsp white vinegar
¼ head green cabbage
1 clove garlic
3 Tbsp unsalted butter
1 bunch flat-leaf parsley
4 eggs
1 Tbsp hot mustard
2 Tbsp Irish whiskey
150ml thickened cream

10 Season the steaks with salt and pepper. Drizzle with vegetable oil. Pour the stout and vinegar into the 3L saucepan and set over a medium heat then season with salt.

9 Place the steaks in the hot frying pan. Shred the cabbage finely.

8 Peel the garlic and slice very finely.

7 Once the stout has come to a simmer, turn the heat to low.

6 Turn the steaks. Add the cabbage and butter to the frying pan. Chop the parsley finely.

5 Break the eggs into the saucepan one at a time.

4 Add the garlic, mustard and parsley to the frying pan.

3 Pour the whiskey into the frying pan, simmer for 30 seconds then add the cream. Season the sauce with salt and pepper.

2 Remove the steaks from the frying pan. Divide the cabbage among serving plates. Carve the steaks and arrange alongside.

1 Use a slotted spoon to remove the poached eggs from the stout and place one on each steak. Pour the sauce over.

PORK

FARMHOUSE PORK SAUSAGES WITH BUTTER BEAN MASH AND TOMATO MAYONNAISE

GEAR
large frying pan
tongs
chopping board
knife
colander
food processor
3L saucepan
wooden spoon
small mixing bowl
whisk

FOOD
8 thick pork sausages
1 Tbsp vegetable oil
2 red onions
2 x 400g cans butter beans
½ cup extra virgin olive oil
salt and pepper
1 tsp truffle oil
¼ cup mayonnaise
1 Tbsp tomato paste
½ bunch dill

10 Place the sausages and vegetable oil in the frying pan and set over a medium heat. Peel the onions.

9 Slice the onions finely and set aside. Drain the cans of butter beans in a colander, then rinse under running water.

8 Add the onions to the frying pan. Place the butter beans and olive oil in the food processor and pulse several times until it forms a coarse mash.

7 Season the butter bean mash with salt and pepper. Place the butter bean mash in the 3L saucepan and set over a medium heat.

6 Turn the sausages.

5 Add the truffle oil to the butter bean mash.

4 Place the mayonnaise and tomato paste in a small mixing bowl and whisk until smooth.

3 Pick the dill sprigs. Turn the sausages.

2 Season the onions with salt and pepper. Spoon the butter bean mash onto four plates.

1 Top the mash with sausages, some onions, and a generous spoon of mayonnaise.

PORK LOIN CHOPS IN CHAR SIU SAUCE WITH CRISPY NOODLE SALAD

Char siu sauce is a Chinese BBQ sauce available in the Asian section of most supermarkets.

FIRST
set the wok of frying oil on medium heat
set the large frying pan on medium heat

GEAR
wok
large frying pan
tongs
chopping board
knife
large mixing bowl
small mixing bowl
pastry brush

FOOD
vegetable oil, for wok-frying
4 x 210g pork loin chops
salt and pepper
1 Tbsp vegetable oil
200g rice vermicelli noodles
2 eschalots
1 cup snow peas
1 cup bean sprouts
1 bunch coriander
2 limes
1 clove garlic
1 red birdseye chilli
1 Tbsp soy sauce
1 tsp fish sauce
½ tsp caster sugar
¼ tsp ground ginger
3 Tbsp char siu sauce

10 Turn the heat under the large frying pan to high. Season the pork chops with salt and pepper, then drizzle with vegetable oil. Place in the frying pan.

9 Place the rice noodles into the wok of hot oil and fry for 1 minute, stirring often, until the oil no longer bubbles and the noodles are crisp. Drain the noodles on absorbent paper.

8 Peel the eschalots and slice finely, then place in the large mixing bowl.

7 Slice the snow peas finely and add to the large mixing bowl. Mix in the sprouts.

6 Turn the pork chops. Roughly tear the coriander and stir into the salad mixture. Cut the limes in half and squeeze the juice into the small mixing bowl.

5 Peel the garlic and mince finely. Slice the chilli finely. Add both to the small bowl.

4 Stir the soy sauce, fish sauce, sugar and ground ginger into the small mixing bowl, stir well, and pour over the salad mixture.

3 Brush the pork chops with char siu sauce on both sides and reduce the heat under the frying pan to medium.

2 Combine the crispy noodles with the salad mixture and divide among four plates.

1 Place a pork chop on each plate and drizzle with pan juices.

BACON AND LEEK OMELETTE
WITH CUCUMBER AND RHUBARB SALAD

No mizuna? Use baby rocket leaves instead.

FIRST
set the grill on high heat

GEAR
large frying pan
2 large mixing bowls
whisk
teaspoon
spatula
tongs
small mixing bowl
stick blender

FOOD
4 rashers rindless bacon
1 Tbsp unsalted butter
1 leek
½ tsp ground fennel seeds
12 eggs
2 Tbsp cream
salt and pepper
1 Lebanese cucumber
1 stick rhubarb
2 cups baby mizuna leaves
¼ bunch dill
¼ cup semi-dried tomatoes in oil
1 lemon
¼ cup extra virgin olive oil

10 Set the large frying pan over a high heat. Slice the bacon finely and place in the pan with the butter.

9 Slice the leek finely and add to the pan. Sprinkle the ground fennel seed over the top.

8 Whisk the eggs and cream in a large mixing bowl and season with salt and pepper. Halve the cucumber lengthways and scrape out the seeds with a teaspoon.

7 Pour the egg mixture into the frying pan, stir with a spatula and reduce the heat to medium. Slice the cucumber very finely and place in the other large mixing bowl.

6 Slice the rhubarb very finely and add to the cucumber along with the mizuna leaves. Stir the egg mixture.

5 Pick the dill and combine with the cucumber salad.

4 Put the semi-dried tomatoes in the small mixing bowl. Cut the lemon in half and squeeze the juice over the tomatoes. Pour in the olive oil. Puree with a stick blender.

3 Place the omelette under the grill. Dress the salad with the tomato sauce.

2 Divide the salad among four plates. Fold the omelette over.

1 Cut the omelette into four and place a piece on each plate.

PORK CUTLETS WITH CARAMELISED PEARS AND ONIONS

FIRST
set the ribbed griddle on high heat

GEAR
ribbed griddle
frying pan
chopping board
knife
vegetable peeler
tongs
wooden spoon

FOOD
4 x 180g pork cutlets
salt and pepper
2 Tbsp vegetable oil
2 red onions
2 firm pears
¼ cup brown sugar
2 Tbsp unsalted butter
½ bunch thyme
½ cup Tokay
2 tsp red wine vinegar
2 Tbsp pistachio dukkah

10 Season the cutlets with salt and pepper then drizzle with vegetable oil. Place on the hot ribbed griddle. Set the frying pan over a high heat. Peel the onions leaving the tails intact, then cut into quarters.

9 Peel the pears and remove the cores. Place the brown sugar and butter in the frying pan and stir well.

8 Cut the pears into quarters. Stir the sugar mixture.

7 Pick the thyme leaves.

6 Place the onions and pears in the frying pan and toss well.

5 Turn the cutlets. Toss the onions.

4 Toss the onions and season lightly with salt and pepper.

3 Add the Tokay and vinegar to the frying pan and stir well.

2 Stir the thyme leaves into the onion mixture. Turn off the heat. Divide the pears and onions among four plates.

1 Place a cutlet on each plate, then drizzle with onion pan juices. Sprinkle with dukkah.

SALAD OF PORK AND FENNEL SAUSAGES WITH ROMAN BEANS AND MARINATED FETA

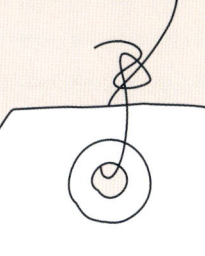

Roman beans are large, olive-green pods in season from May until November. They are a bit thicker, and require more cooking than most other beans.

FIRST
boil 2L water in kettle

GEAR
3L saucepan
frying pan
chopping board
knife
tongs
large mixing bowl
small mixing bowl

FOOD
2L boiling water
300g Roman beans
4 thick pork and fennel sausages
1 punnet cherry tomatoes
1 bunch rocket
1 bunch tarragon
2 lemons
2 Tbsp extra virgin olive oil
2 tsp balsamic vinegar
150g marinated feta cheese

10 Fill the 3L saucepan with the boiling water and set over a high heat. Set the frying pan over a high heat. Top and tail the Roman beans.

9 Place the sausages in the hot frying pan. Cut the tomatoes into quarters and place in the large mixing bowl.

8 Tear the rocket into small pieces and place in the large mixing bowl.

7 Pick the tarragon leaves and add to the rocket.

6 Place the beans in the boiling water

5 Cut the lemons in half and squeeze the juice into the small bowl. Stir in the olive oil and balsamic vinegar, then season with salt and pepper.

4 Turn the sausages.

3 Remove the beans from the boiling water and cut in half.

2 Remove the sausages from the frying pan and cut into small pieces. Add the beans, sausages and dressing to the large mixing bowl, toss well. Divide the salad among four plates.

1 Crumble the feta over the top.

CHARGRILLED PORK FILLET AND YABBIES WITH APPLE AND CHICKPEA SALAD

FIRST
set the ribbed griddle or BBQ grill on high heat

GEAR
ribbed griddle or BBQ grill
colander
chopping board
knife
teaspoon
frying pan
apple corer
tongs
mandoline slicer
large mixing bowl

FOOD
2 x 300g pork tenderloins
salt and pepper
2 tsp sesame oil
400g can chickpeas
8 yabbies
1 Tbsp extra virgin olive oil
2 Granny Smith apples
2 limes
½ cup roasted red capsicums
¼ bunch mint
2 Tbsp sesame seeds
1 Tbsp avocado oil
2 Tbsp redcurrant jelly

10 Season the pork tenderloins with salt and pepper then drizzle with sesame oil. Place on the hot ribbed griddle. Drain the chickpeas in a colander and rinse well under running water.

9 Split the yabbies with a large sharp knife and scrape out the intestinal tract with a teaspoon. Season with salt and pepper, then drizzle with olive oil. Set the frying pan over a high heat.

8 Core the apples and slice finely with a mandoline slicer. Place in the large mixing bowl. Cut the limes in half and squeeze the juice over the apple slices. Toss well.

7 Cut the roasted capsicums into fine slices and combine with the apples.

6 Turn the pork. Pick the mint leaves and place in the salad bowl.

5 Arrange the yabbies on the ribbed griddle. Pour the sesame seeds into the hot frying pan and cook, tossing constantly, until golden, then transfer to the salad bowl. Add the chickpeas to the salad bowl.

4 Drizzle the avocado oil over the salad and season with salt and pepper.

3 Turn the yabbies. Brush the pork with redcurrant jelly.

2 Remove the pork from the griddle and slice finely. Add to the salad and toss well. Divide salad among four plates.

1 Garnish with yabbies.

WOK-SEARED PORK FILLET WITH HOKKIEN NOODLES AND GINGER

FIRST
set the wok on high heat

GEAR
wok
chopping board
knife
large mixing bowl
wooden spoon
vegetable peeler
mandoline slicer
tongs
small mixing bowl

FOOD
2 x 300g pork tenderloins
2 tsp Chinese five spice
½ cup cornflour
salt and pepper
¼ cup peanut oil
2 carrots
2 cups sugar snap peas
1 bunch choy sum
1 medium piece ginger
400g hokkien noodles
1 bunch basil
¼ bunch Vietnamese mint
½ cup peanuts
1 cup chicken stock
3 Tbsp dark soy sauce
1 Tbsp fish sauce
1 Tbsp honey

10 Slice the pork into 2cm-thick pieces and toss in five spice, cornflour, salt and pepper in the large mixing bowl. Pour the peanut oil into the hot wok.

9 Place the pork in the wok and stir well. Peel the carrots and slice finely on the mandoline.

8 Toss the pork. Top and tail the sugar snap peas. Cut the choy sum into halves.

7 Cut the ginger into very fine batons.

6 Add the carrots and hokkien noodles to the wok and toss well.

5 Stir the ginger into the wok. Pick the basil and Vietnamese mint leaves.

4 Place the sugar snap peas and choy sum in the wok. Chop the peanuts.

3 Pour the chicken stock, soy sauce, fish sauce and honey into the wok.

2 Stir in the herbs.

1 Divide the stir fry among four bowls and top with peanuts.

Vietnamese mint is a strongly flavoured sour herb that can be found in some supermarkets and most Asian grocers. Feel free to adjust the amount, it packs some punch!

GAMMON STEAKS WITH CRISP HERBED POTATOES AND IRISH GRAVY

FIRST
set the 5L saucepan of deep-frying oil on medium heat
set the ribbed griddle or BBQ grill on high heat

GEAR
5L saucepan
ribbed griddle
3L saucepan
vegetable peeler
tongs
chopping board
knife
mandoline slicer
whisk
mortar and pestle

FOOD
vegetable oil, for deep-frying
1 cup Guinness
4 large potatoes
1 Tbsp gravy powder
4 x 160g rindless gammon steaks
cooking oil spray
½ bunch sage
2 Tbsp fine salt

10 Pour the Guinness into the 3L saucepan and set over a medium heat. Peel the potatoes.

9 Whisk the gravy powder into the Guinness and bring to a simmer. Slice the potatoes as thinly as possible using the mandoline slicer.

8 Begin frying the potato slices in small batches in the saucepan of hot oil. Once golden and crisp, drain on absorbent paper.

7 Continue batch-frying potatoes. Spray the gammon steaks with cooking oil and place on the hot ribbed griddle.

6 Continue batch-frying potatoes. Pick the sage leaves and place in the mortar.

5 Continue batch-frying potatoes. Add the salt to the mortar and pound until it forms a smooth herb salt.

4 Continue batch-frying potatoes. Turn the gammon steaks.

3 Once the gravy has thickened, season lightly with salt.

2 Dust the crisp potatoes with sage salt and arrange on four plates.

1 Place the gammon steaks next to the potatoes and top with gravy.

Gammon is a traditional Irish ham made on the bone. It is very tender and slightly salty. Ask your butcher, he'll help you out.

PORK MEATBALLS WITH CREAMY TOMATO SAUCE AND FRIED ITALIAN BREAD

GEAR
2 frying pans
large mixing bowl
chopping board
knife
tongs
wooden spoon
slotted spoon

FOOD
1 clove garlic
600g pork mince
2 Tbsp tomato paste
3 eggs
1 Tbsp dried marjoram
2 tsp dried rosemary
salt and pepper
¼ cup extra virgin olive oil
½ cup vegetable oil
½ loaf crusty Italian bread
½ bunch basil
2 cups tomato passata
1 tsp brown sugar
1 tsp red wine vinegar
150ml double cream
120g Parmesan cheese

10 Set the two frying pans over a high heat. Peel the garlic and chop finely, then place in the large mixing bowl. Add the pork mince, tomato paste, eggs, marjoram and rosemary.

9 Season the meatball mixture with salt and pepper then mix thoroughly. Form into golf ball-sized balls using damp hands.

8 Pour the olive oil into one hot frying pan and add the meatballs.

7 Pour the vegetable oil into the second hot frying pan.

6 Tear the bread into small chunks and fry in the hot vegetable oil until golden brown. Remove bread with a slotted spoon and drain on absorbent paper.

5 Turn the meatballs. Pick the basil leaves.

4 Add the passata, sugar and vinegar to the meatballs. Season the sauce with salt and pepper.

3 Stir the cream into the tomato sauce. Grate the Parmesan.

2 Gently mix the basil leaves into the meatball pan. Divide the fried bread among four bowls.

1 Place the meatballs and sauce on top of the bread then garnish with grated Parmesan.

SWEET AND SOUR PORK IN GINGER MARMALADE

FIRST
set the wok on high heat
boil 2L water in kettle

GEAR
wok
chopping board
knife
wooden spoon
large mixing bowl

FOOD
2 x 300g pork tenderloins
2 Tbsp plain flour
salt and pepper
2 Tbsp vegetable oil
1 brown onion
2 sticks celery
1 red capsicum
200g rice vermicelli noodles
2L boiling water
4 cloves garlic
½ cup cashews
¼ cup ginger marmalade
½ cup liquid chicken stock
1 Tbsp white vinegar
1 bunch mint

10 Slice the pork into 2cm pieces and dust with flour, salt and pepper.

9 Pour the vegetable oil into the wok and add the pork pieces. Peel the onion and slice finely.

8 Slice the celery and capsicum into fine strips. Stir the pork.

7 Place the rice noodles into the large mixing bowl and pour the boiling water over. Set aside to steep. Peel the garlic and slice finely.

6 Mix the vegetables into the wok.

5 Stir in the garlic. Chop the cashews.

4 Add the marmalade and chicken stock to the wok. Stir well.

3 Stir the vinegar into the pork mixture. Pick the mint leaves.

2 Drain the rice noodles and divide among four bowls. Stir the mint leaves into the wok.

1 Spoon the sweet and sour pork over the noodles, and top with marmalade sauce and cashews.

PORK CUTLETS WITH COGNAC RASPBERRY SAUCE AND CELERY SALAD

The flavour of good cognac will certainly help this dish, but if you've got a bottle of brandy hanging around, feel free to use it instead.

FIRST
set the frying pan on high heat

GEAR
frying pan
chopping board
knife
3L saucepan
hand grater
mortar and pestle
large mixing bowl

FOOD
4 x 210g pork cutlets
salt and pepper
1 Tbsp vegetable oil
1 eschalot
¼ cup poppy seeds
1 orange
¼ bunch thyme
¼ cup extra virgin olive oil
1 tsp sherry vinegar
4 sticks celery
1 bunch parsley
¼ cup cognac
2 punnets raspberries
150ml thickened cream
½ chicken stock cube

10 Season the cutlets with salt and pepper, then drizzle with vegetable oil and place in the hot frying pan. Peel the eschalot and dice finely.

9 Place the poppy seeds in the 3L saucepan and set over a high heat. Finely grate the zest of the orange and place in the mortar.

8 Stir the poppy seeds. Pick the thyme.

7 Pour the poppy seeds and thyme into the mortar and pound until the seeds crack.

6 Halve the orange and squeeze the juice into the mortar. Add the olive oil and vinegar, and stir well. Season with salt and pepper.

5 Turn the pork cutlets. Slice the celery finely and place in the large mixing bowl.

4 Chop the parsley and add to the celery, then pour the poppy seed dressing over the top.

3 Pour the cognac, raspberries and eschalot into the frying pan, stir briefly, then add the cream and stock cube. Turn the heat to medium.

2 Divide the salad among four plates.

1 Place a cutlet on each plate and top with the pan sauce.

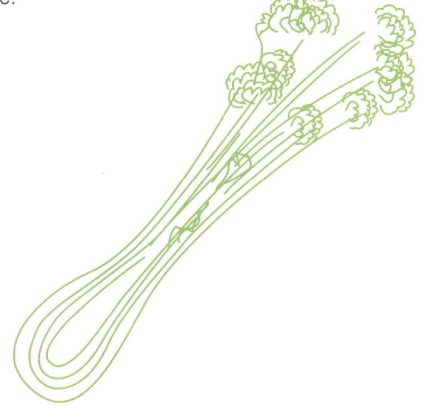

PISTACHIO-CRUSTED PORK CUTLETS WITH GRILLED BABY CORN SALAD

You can adapt this recipe for most nuts and most meats. Design a flavour match that suits your style.

FIRST
set the ribbed griddle or
  BBQ grill on high heat
set the grill to high

GEAR
ribbed griddle or BBQ grill
frying pan
chopping board
knife
tongs
food processor
baking tray
large mixing bowl

FOOD
4 x 210g pork cutlets
salt and pepper
2 Tbsp vegetable oil
3 punnets baby corn
½ tsp ground cardamom
¼ tsp ground nutmeg
¼ tsp ground white pepper
1 Tbsp extra virgin olive oil
200g pistachios
¼ bunch parsley
½ cup breadcrumbs
3 egg whites
2 cups baby spinach leaves
2 long red chillies
1 Tbsp cider vinegar
1 lemon

10 Season the pork cutlets with salt and pepper then drizzle with vegetable oil and arrange on the hot ribbed griddle. Cut the baby corn in half lengthways.

9 Toss the corn pieces in cardamom, nutmeg, white pepper, salt and olive oil then arrange on the ribbed griddle.

8 Place the pistachios, parsley and breadcrumbs in a food processor and pulse until it forms coarse crumbs. Add the egg whites and pulse several times to bring the mixture together.

7 Place the spinach leaves in the large mixing bowl. Slice the chillies finely and add to the bowl.

6 Add the corn to the spinach leaves, sprinkle with cider vinegar, and toss well.

5 Turn the pork cutlets.

4 Press the pistachio paste onto the cutlets.

3 Divide the salad among four plates. Transfer the cutlets to a baking tray and place under the grill.

2 Cut the lemon into quarters and place one on each plate.

1 Place the cutlets next to the salad.

CHICKEN & POULTRY

PIRI-PIRI CHICKEN DRUMETTES WITH ZUCCHINI FRITTERS AND AVOCADO

FIRST
set the 5L saucepan on high heat

GEAR
5L saucepan with fitting lid
chopping board
knife
box grater
2 large mixing bowls
wooden spoon
frying pan
slotted lifter
large kitchen spoon

FOOD
2 lemons
1kg chicken drumettes
salt and pepper
1 Tbsp chilli flakes
1 tsp garlic powder
1 tsp ground cumin
½ tsp ground coriander
2 Tbsp extra virgin olive oil
4 large zucchini
2 Tbsp plain flour
2 eggs
½ cup grated mozzarella cheese
1 Tbsp vegetable oil
1 cup chicken stock
2 Tbsp bourbon whiskey
½ bunch oregano leaves
2 avocados

10 Finely grate the lemon zest and place in a large mixing bowl. Add the chicken and season with salt and pepper then toss in the spices.

9 Pour the olive oil into the hot 5L saucepan and add the spiced chicken. Shred the zucchini on the coarse blade of a box grater into the second large mixing bowl. Set the frying pan over a medium heat.

8 Stir the flour, eggs and mozzarella into the zucchini, season with salt and pepper and mix thoroughly. Pour the vegetable oil into the frying pan. Toss the chicken pieces.

7 Place eight large spoons of zucchini mixture into the hot frying pan and flatten into disc shapes. Toss the chicken pieces.

6 Add the chicken stock and bourbon to the saucepan and fit the lid.

5 Turn the zucchini fritters.

4 Pick the oregano leaves.

3 Split the avocados and remove the seeds. Use a large spoon to remove the flesh.

2 Place a zucchini fritter on each of four plates. Slice the avocados into fans and arrange on top of the fritters.

1 Arrange the chicken drumettes around the fritters and garnish with oregano leaves.

CHARGRILLED SKEWERS OF CHICKEN AND SOURDOUGH WITH CHILLI-LIME BASTE

FIRST
set the ribbed griddle or
  BBQ grill on medium heat

GEAR
ribbed griddle or BBQ grill
chopping board
knife
large mixing bowl
8 metal skewers
2 small mixing bowls
pastry brush

FOOD
600g chicken thigh fillet
salt and pepper
½ loaf sourdough bread
cooking oil spray
4 limes
¼ cup sweet chilli sauce
1 Tbsp fish sauce
1 Tbsp soy sauce
1 bunch watercress
1 red capsicum
2 tsp tarragon vinegar
1 Tbsp avocado oil

10 Slice the thigh fillet into 1cm-wide strips, then season with salt and pepper.

9 Cut the bread into 2cm cubes. Begin to pierce the chicken onto skewers, alternating with cubes of bread.

8 Finish skewering the chicken. Spray the skewers with cooking oil then arrange on the hot ribbed griddle.

7 Cut the limes in half and squeeze the juice into a small mixing bowl.

6 Stir the chilli sauce, fish sauce and soy sauce into the lime juice.

5 Turn the skewers. Pick the watercress sprigs and place in the second small mixing bowl.

4 Dice the capsicum finely and combine with the watercress. Season with salt and pepper, then drizzle with tarragon vinegar and avocado oil.

3 Arrange the watercress salad on four plates. Baste the chicken skewers with the chilli-lime sauce.

2 Baste the skewers again.

1 Baste the skewers then arrange them next to the watercress salad and drizzle with a little extra sauce.

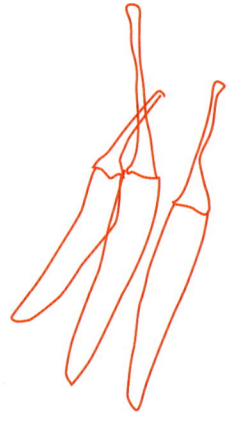

LARB GAI: SPICY THAI CHICKEN SALAD

GEAR
wok
chopping board
knife
wooden spoon
large mixing bowl
box grater

FOOD
2 eschalots
2 cloves garlic
3cm piece ginger
2 Tbsp peanut oil
1 tsp fine salt
600g chicken mince
1 stick lemon grass
4 shallots
3 Tbsp red curry paste
½ bunch coriander
4 kaffir lime leaves
¼ cup coconut cream
2 Tbsp fish sauce
1 cup bean sprouts
¼ cup peanuts

10 Set the wok over a high heat. Peel the eschalots and slice finely. Place the eschalots in the large mixing bowl.

9 Peel the garlic and slice finely then place in the large mixing bowl. Grate the ginger finely into the bowl.

8 Pour the oil and salt into the wok then add the chicken mince. Stir well to break up. Cut the green portion off the lemon grass, then slice the white part finely and add to the mixing bowl.

7 Stir the chicken. Slice the shallots finely and add to the salad.

6 Spoon the curry paste into the wok and stir well. Pick the coriander leaves and add to the salad.

5 Slice the lime leaves very finely and mix into the chicken, then pour in the coconut cream and fish sauce.

4 Mix the bean sprouts into the salad.

3 Chop the peanuts finely.

2 Adjust the seasoning in the chicken as needed with salt, then combine through the salad.

1 Divide the larb gai among four plates, then top with chopped peanuts.

CHICKEN BREAST IN RIESLING AND CREAM WITH EXOTIC MUSHROOMS

FIRST
set the ribbed griddle or BBQ grill on high heat

GEAR
ribbed griddle or BBQ grill
chopping board
knife
tongs
frying pan
vegetable peeler
box grater

FOOD
4 x 180g skinless chicken breasts
salt and pepper
cooking oil spray
1 brown onion
2 Tbsp unsalted butter
2 cloves garlic
1 turnip
1 punnet shiitake mushrooms
1 punnet shimeji mushrooms
1 bunch thyme
1 tsp honey
250ml Riesling
300ml thickened cream
¼ tsp ground nutmeg

10 Season the chicken breasts with salt and pepper and spray with cooking oil. Arrange on the hot ribbed griddle. Set the large frying pan over a high heat. Peel the onion and dice finely.

9 Place the onion and butter in the frying pan. Peel the garlic and slice finely then add to the onion.

8 Peel the turnip and shred coarsely on a box grater, then add to the frying pan. Stir well.

7 Turn the chicken breasts. Slice the shiitake mushrooms ½-cm thick, and separate the shimeji mushrooms. Stir both mushrooms into the frying pan.

6 Chop the thyme finely and mix with the mushrooms.

5 Pour the honey and wine into the frying pan and season with salt and pepper.

4 Pour the cream into the frying pan and stir thoroughly.

3 Remove the chicken from the ribbed griddle and halve lengthways. Place the sliced chicken into the frying pan and mix to ensure the meat is immersed in the sauce.

2 Sprinkle in the nutmeg and stir well.

1 Transfer the chicken from the frying pan to the chopping board. Divide the mushroom mixture and sauce among four plates. Arrange the chicken on top, sliced or whole as you prefer.

GRILLED CHICKEN THIGHS WITH RADICCHIO, POTATOES AND SAGE

FIRST
set the ribbed griddle or
  BBQ grill on high heat

GEAR
ribbed griddle or BBQ grill
chopping board
knife
tongs
2 large mixing bowls

FOOD
8 chicken thigh fillets
1 tsp celery salt
¼ cup extra virgin olive oil
2 large washed potatoes
2 Tbsp vegetable oil
salt and pepper
1 head radicchio
½ cup green beans
2 bunches sage
1 Tbsp cider vinegar
½ cup ricotta cheese

10 Dust the chicken pieces in celery salt and pepper, then drizzle with half the olive oil. Arrange on the hot griddle.

9 Slice the potatoes ½-cm thick then place in the large mixing bowl. Toss in vegetable oil, salt and pepper. Arrange on the hot griddle.

8 Tear the radicchio into small pieces and place in the second mixing bowl.

7 Slice the beans into fine strips and add to the radicchio.

6 Turn the chicken pieces. Pick the sage leaves and mix with the salad.

5 Turn the potatoes.

4 Toss the salad with the remaining olive oil and the vinegar. Season with salt and pepper.

3 Turn the chicken.

2 Remove the potatoes from the ribbed griddle and toss through the salad. Divide the salad among four plates and top with crumbled ricotta.

1 Carve the chicken pieces and arrange next to the salad.

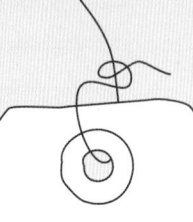

Radicchio is a bright red bitter leaf vegetable from northern Italy. Red oak leaf lettuce is a good substitute.

BBQ CHICKEN RICE PAPER ROLLS WITH HOI SIN AND ESCHALOTS

FIRST
boil 1L water in kettle

GEAR
chopping board
knife
3 large mixing bowls
vegetable peeler
wooden spoon
tongs
box grater
colander
scissors

FOOD
½ BBQ chicken
100g rice vermicelli noodles
1L boiling water
1 carrot
4 eschalots
½ bunch mint
½ bunch coriander
2 red birdseye chillies
1 lime
1 Tbsp fish sauce
2 Tbsp soy sauce
½ tsp caster sugar
2L tepid water
16 sheets rice paper
¼ cup hoi sin sauce
chilli sauce, to serve

10 Pull the meat off the chicken and shred into fine pieces. Place in a large mixing bowl.

9 Place the rice noodles and 1L boiling water in a second mixing bowl and set aside. Peel the carrot and shred on the coarse blade of a box grater into the chicken bowl.

8 Peel the eschalots and slice finely, then add to the chicken.

7 Roughly pick the herbs and add to the salad mixture. Slice the chillies very finely and toss in.

6 Cut the lime in half and squeeze the juice into the salad. Pour in the fish sauce, soy sauce and sugar then mix thoroughly.

5 Drain the noodles in the colander then snip into 10cm lengths with the scissors. Mix into the salad.

4 Pour the 2L tepid water into the third large mixing bowl and add the rice paper sheets one at a time.

3 Arrange the softened rice paper sheets on the bench and brush with hoi sin sauce.

2 Divide the chicken mixture among the sheets in a cylindrical mound at one end. To roll up, fold in the sides then roll up to seal.

1 Finish assembling the rice paper rolls then spoon some chilli sauce into ramekins and divide among four plates.

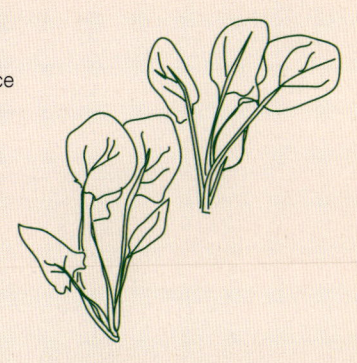

MOROCCAN-SPICED SPATCHCOCK ON COUSCOUS WITH ORANGES AND LEMONS

You can use chicken pieces instead for this recipe, but the cooking time will be a little longer.

FIRST
set the ribbed griddle or BBQ grill on high heat
boil 500ml water in kettle
half-fill the 3L saucepan with water and set to simmer

GEAR
ribbed griddle or BBQ grill
2 large mixing bowls
chopping board
knife
3L saucepan
whisk

FOOD
4 x size 5 butterflied spatchcocks
2 tsp paprika
2 tsp turmeric
1 tsp ground cumin
1 tsp ground cinnamon
½ tsp ground coriander
½ tsp ground chilli
2 Tbsp extra virgin olive oil
salt and pepper
500g couscous
2 Tbsp unsalted butter
500ml boiling water
2 oranges
2 lemons
½ bunch coriander
4 Tbsp sliced almonds

10 Place the spatchcocks in a large mixing bowl and top with the spices and olive oil. Season with salt and pepper then arrange on the hot ribbed griddle. Cover lightly with foil.

9 Place the couscous in the second large mixing bowl with the butter and a generous pinch of salt. Pour in the boiling water and whisk through. Set over the 3L saucepan of simmering water.

8 Peel the oranges.

7 Peel the lemons. Stir the couscous.

6 Slice the citrus fruits finely and cut into small pieces.

5 Turn the spatchcocks and cover again with foil. Pick the coriander leaves.

4 Stir the couscous.

3 Add the diced citrus, coriander and almonds to the couscous and season lightly with salt and pepper.

2 Divide the couscous among four plates.

1 Halve the spatchcocks and arrange on top.

CHICKEN & POULTRY

LEMON CHICKEN AND AVOCADO QUESADILLAS

FIRST
turn the sandwich press on

GEAR
chopping board
knife
frying pan
wooden spoon
2 large mixing bowls
kitchen spoon
whisk
vegetable peeler

FOOD
400g smoked chicken breast
2 lemons
2 Tbsp honey
1 tsp white vinegar
2 avocados
¼ cup sour cream
1 tsp ground cumin
1 tsp chilli flakes
salt and pepper
1 red onion
8 large tortillas
1 bunch rocket
1 cup grated mozzarella cheese
2 bunches asparagus
½ bunch flat-leaf parsley
1 Tbsp extra virgin olive oil
2 tsp balsamic vinegar

10 Slice the smoked chicken into ½-cm-thick pieces. Cut the lemons in half and squeeze the juice into the frying pan. Add the chicken, honey and vinegar and set over a high heat.

9 Halve the avocados, remove the seeds, and scoop the flesh into a large mixing bowl using a kitchen spoon. Stir the chicken.

8 Add the sour cream and spices to the avocados and season generously with salt and pepper. Beat thoroughly with a whisk until it forms a smooth mixture.

7 Peel the onion and slice very finely. Remove the chicken from the frying pan.

6 Lay the tortillas on the bench and smear half with avocado puree.

5 Assemble the chicken, onion, rocket and cheese on the avocado, place the remaining tortillas on top and place in the hot sandwich press.

4 Strip the asparagus into long pieces with a vegetable peeler and place in the second large mixing bowl.

3 Pick the parsley leaves and add to the asparagus. Drizzle with olive oil and balsamic vinegar and season with salt and pepper.

2 Arrange the salad on four plates.

1 Halve the quesadillas and place next to the salad.

CHICKEN SOBA NOODLE SALAD WITH PONZU DRESSING

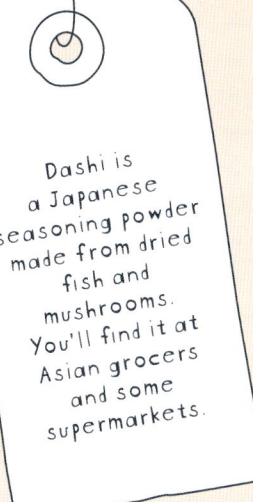

Dashi is a Japanese seasoning powder made from dried fish and mushrooms. You'll find it at Asian grocers and some supermarkets.

FIRST
boil 2L water in kettle
set the frying pan on medium heat

GEAR
chopping board
knife
frying pan
large mixing bowl
3L saucepan
colander
tongs
wooden spoon
1L saucepan
fine sieve

FOOD
400g chicken thigh fillet
1 Tbsp sesame oil
4 heads bok choy
6 shallots
½ cup snowpeas
2L boiling water
½ cup water chestnuts
200g soba noodles
2 Tbsp mirin
1 Tbsp rice vinegar
2 Tbsp soy sauce
1 tsp dashi powder
2 lemons
½ bunch coriander
250ml liquid chicken stock

10 Slice the chicken finely and place in the frying pan with the sesame oil. Shred the bok choy finely and place in the large mixing bowl.

9 Slice the shallots and snowpeas finely and add to the bok choy.

8 Pour the boiling water into the 3L saucepan and set over a high heat. Halve the water chestnuts and add to the large mixing bowl.

7 Put the soba noodles in the boiling water and stir well. Turn the chicken.

6 Pour the mirin, rice vinegar, soy sauce and dashi powder into the 1L saucepan.

5 Finely grate the lemon zest into the 1L saucepan, then halve the lemons and squeeze the juice in. Set over a high heat.

4 Pick the coriander leaves and add to the salad.

3 Drain the noodles in a colander and refresh under cold water. Drain well and toss in the salad. Turn the chicken and pour the stock into the frying pan.

2 Strain the ponzu dressing through a fine sieve into the salad and mix well.

1 Slice the chicken finely, add to the salad and divide among four plates.

FIVE SPICE DUCK BREAST WITH CAULIFLOWER AND GORGONZOLA PUREE

FIRST
boil 2L water in kettle

GEAR
frying pan
chopping board
knife
3L saucepan
tongs
large mixing bowl
small mixing bowl
colander
food processor

FOOD
4 x 150g duck breast
1 tsp Chinese five spice
salt and pepper
1 tsp vegetable oil
2L boiling water
1 head cauliflower
1 egg
1 eschalot
½ bunch watercress
2 Tbsp pine nuts
1 lemon
1 tsp capers
2 Tbsp extra virgin olive oil
120g gorgonzola cheese

10 Set the large frying pan over a medium heat. Score the duck breasts lightly and season with five spice, salt and pepper. Pour the vegetable oil into the frying pan and arrange the duck skin-side down in the pan.

9 Place the 3L saucepan on the stove and pour in 2L boiling water. Add a teaspoon of salt. Cut the florets off the cauliflower and place in the saucepan.

8 Put the egg in the saucepan. Peel the eschalot and dice finely.

7 Turn the heat under the frying pan to high. Baste the duck breasts with the pan juices.

6 Pick the watercress into large sprigs and place in the large mixing bowl with the pine nuts.

5 Finely grate the lemon zest into the large mixing bowl, then cut the lemon in half and squeeze the juice into a small bowl. Baste the duck breasts with the pan juices.

4 Chop the capers and add to the lemon juice. Stir in the olive oil.

3 Turn the duck over and baste with pan juices. Drain the cauliflower and egg in a colander. Place the cauliflower in a food processor with the gorgonzola and eschalot and pulse until smooth. Season with salt.

2 Cut the boiled egg in half and scoop the filling into the small bowl. Mix well and season with salt and a generous amount of black pepper. Spoon the cauliflower puree onto four plates.

1 Carve the duck and lay on top of the puree. Toss the watercress through the egg mixture and lay alongside.

BARBECUED QUAILS WITH PROSCIUTTO, PEAR AND BASIL SALAD

Butterflying is not the easiest technique to master, so why not get your butcher to do the hard work for you.

FIRST
set the ribbed griddle or BBQ grill on high heat
set the grill on high

GEAR
ribbed griddle or BBQ grill
chopping board
knife
tongs
baking tray
large mixing bowl
mandoline slicer
food processor

FOOD
4 jumbo butterflied quails
salt and pepper
1 Tbsp vegetable oil
¼ cup peeled hazelnuts
1 Tbsp sesame seeds
2 Tbsp sunflower seeds
½ bunch sage
¼ tsp ground cumin
¼ tsp ground allspice
4 slices prosciutto
1 pear
1 fennel
1 bunch basil
2 Tbsp extra virgin olive oil
1 Tbsp sherry vinegar

10 Season the quails with salt and pepper and drizzle with vegetable oil. Arrange the quails on the hot ribbed griddle. Combine the hazelnuts, sesame seeds and sunflower seeds on a baking tray and set under the grill.

9 Stir the hazelnut mixture. Pick the sage leaves.

8 Transfer the nut mixture to a food processor and pulse until it forms coarse crumbs. Chop the sage finely and stir into the nuts along with the spices. Season with salt and pepper.

7 Turn the quails. Tear the prosciutto into fine pieces and place in the large mixing bowl.

6 Halve the pear and remove the seeds, then shave on a mandoline. Transfer to the large mixing bowl.

5 Shave the fennel finely and combine with the pear.

4 Turn the quails again. Pick the basil leaves and toss thoroughly with the fennel mixture.

3 Dress the salad with olive oil and sherry vinegar then season lightly with salt and pepper.

2 Turn the quails again. Divide the salad among four plates.

1 Halve the quails and arrange next to the salad. Top with the nut mixture.

CHICKEN & POULTRY

CHICKEN AND SAUSAGE JAMBALAYA

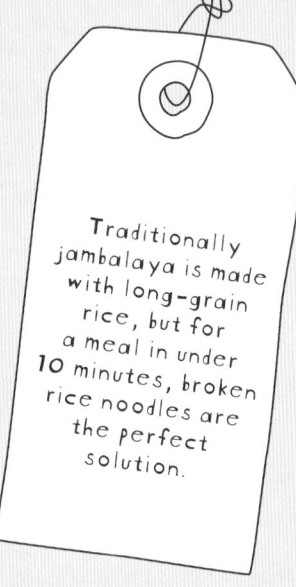

Traditionally jambalaya is made with long-grain rice, but for a meal in under 10 minutes, broken rice noodles are the perfect solution.

FIRST
boil 2L water in kettle
set the 5L saucepan on
   medium heat

GEAR
5L saucepan
3L saucepan
wooden spoon
box grater
vegetable peeler
colander

FOOD
400g chicken thigh fillet
2 Tbsp vegetable oil
2 Tbsp Cajun seasoning
2L boiling water
2 chicken stock cubes
2 chorizo sausages
2 red onions
2 green capsicums
200g rice noodles
4 vine-ripened tomatoes
½ bunch thyme
½ bunch oregano
salt and pepper
½ cup sherry

10 Slice the chicken into thick strips and place in the hot 5L saucepan with the vegetable oil and Cajun seasoning.

9 Pour the boiling water and chicken stock cubes into the 3L saucepan and set over a high heat. Slice the sausages finely and add to the chicken. Stir well.

8 Peel the onions and slice finely. Add to the chicken mixture.

7 Dice the capsicums. Add to the chicken mixture.

6 Break the noodles into small pieces and add to the boiling chicken stock.

5 Dice the tomatoes into small pieces and stir into the chicken mixture.

4 Chop the thyme and oregano finely and set aside.

3 Season the chicken mixture with salt and pepper.

2 Drain the noodles, reserving the chicken stock. Add the noodles to the chicken mixture and pour in enough of the stock to make a thick stew consistency.

1 Stir in the herbs and sherry then divide among four bowls.

PASTA

VERMICELLI WITH PANCETTA, BEETROOT AND HORSERADISH

FIRST
boil 4L water in kettle

GEAR
5L saucepan
frying pan
chopping board
knife
wooden spoon
vegetable peeler
box grater
colander
tongs

FOOD
4L boiling water
2 tsp fine salt
150g pancetta
¼ cup extra virgin olive oil
2 large beetroot
2 cloves garlic
500g dried vermicelli (4 minute)
½ cup port
½ cup liquid vegetable stock
2 tsp minced horseradish
1 bunch sage
¼ cup pitted Kalamata olives
½ cup feta cheese

10 Set the 5L saucepan over a high heat then add the boiling water and the fine salt. Set a frying pan over a high heat. Dice the pancetta finely.

9 Place the pancetta and olive oil in the frying pan. Peel the beetroot.

8 Stir the pancetta. Grate the beetroot coarsely and add the the pancetta.

7 Peel the garlic and slice finely then stir into the frying pan.

6 Place the vermicelli into the boiling water and stir well. Pour the port into the frying pan.

5 Add the vegetable stock and horseradish to the frying pan. Stir the vermicelli.

4 Pick the sage leaves.

3 Chop the olives.

2 Drain the pasta thoroughly in a colander then return to the saucepan. Pour the beetroot mixture over the top.

1 Mix the sage and olives into the pasta, then crumble in the feta. Divide among four plates.

Pancetta comes in two styles, round and flat. Flat pancetta is much easier for dicing, has a firmer consistency and less saltiness.

SMOKED CHICKEN PASTA SALAD WITH WALNUTS AND WATERCRESS

FIRST
boil 4L water in kettle

GEAR
5L saucepan
chopping board
knife
large mixing bowl
tongs
wooden spoon
colander
box grater
small mixing bowl

FOOD
4L boiling water
2 tsp fine salt
500g dried angel hair pasta
 (4 minute)
250g smoked chicken breast
½ cup walnuts
2 Tbsp capers
2 eschalots
½ bunch watercress
120g provolone cheese
¼ cup mayonnaise
¼ cup natural yoghurt
2 Tbsp horseradish cream
2 tsp ground fennel seeds
salt and pepper

10 Set the 5L saucepan over a high heat. Pour in the boiling water then add the salt and pasta. Stir well.

9 Shred the smoked chicken breast into very fine pieces and place in the large mixing bowl.

8 Roughly crush the walnuts and add to the chicken with the capers.

7 Peel the eschalots and slice very finely. Stir into the chicken mixture.

6 Drain the pasta in a colander and rinse under running water to cool. Shake well to drain thoroughly.

5 Pick the watercress into small sprigs and add to the chicken mixture.

4 Shred the provolone on the coarse blade of the box grater and fold into the chicken mixture.

3 Combine the mayonnaise, yoghurt, horseradish cream and fennel seeds in the small mixing bowl.

2 Season the chicken mixture with salt and pepper then stir in the mayonnaise dressing.

1 Toss in the pasta and mix thoroughly. Divide salad among four plates.

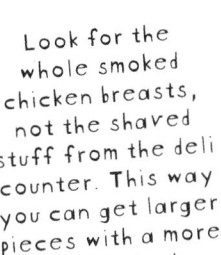

Look for the whole smoked chicken breasts, not the shaved stuff from the deli counter. This way you can get larger pieces with a more elegant look.

ANGEL HAIR PASTA WITH WALNUT SAUCE AND RICOTTA

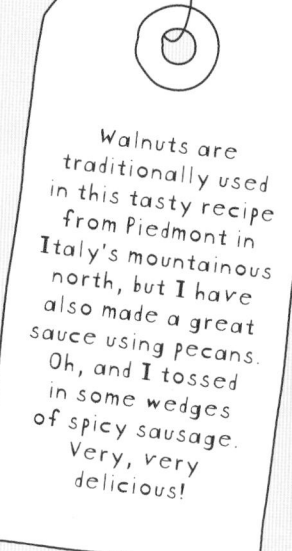

Walnuts are traditionally used in this tasty recipe from Piedmont in Italy's mountainous north, but I have also made a great sauce using pecans. Oh, and I tossed in some wedges of spicy sausage. Very, very delicious!

FIRST
boil 4L water in kettle
set the grill on high

GEAR
5L saucepan
3L saucepan
chopping board
baking tray
knife
wooden spoon
food processor
tongs
colander

FOOD
4L boiling water
2 tsp fine salt
500ml milk
½ cup Marsala wine
1 chicken stock cube
300g walnuts
½ bunch thyme
1 clove garlic
salt and pepper
800g dried angel hair pasta (4 minute)
½ bunch flat-leaf parsley
1 lemon
300g ricotta cheese
2 Tbsp extra virgin olive oil

10 Set the 5L saucepan over a high heat then add the boiling water and fine salt. Pour the milk and Marsala into the 3L saucepan, crumble in the stock cube and set over a high heat.

9 Scatter the walnuts on a baking tray, place under the grill and cook for a couple of minutes until lightly toasted.

8 Pick the thyme leaves and set aside.

7 Once the milk mixture comes to the boil, turn the heat to medium and add the walnuts and thyme.

6 Peel the garlic and slice finely, then add to the walnut mixture. Season with salt and pepper.

5 Put the pasta in the boiling water and stir well.

4 Pick the parsley leaves and chop finely.

3 Transfer the walnut mixture to the food processor and pulse several times until it forms a coarse sauce. Return the sauce to the 3L saucepan and set over a low heat.

2 Cut the lemon into quarters.

1 Drain the pasta thoroughly in a colander and toss through the sauce. Crumble in the ricotta and divide among four plates. Garnish with the parsley, lemon wedges and olive oil.

SPINACH AND RICOTTA RAVIOLI WITH FRIED CAPERS AND GARLIC

FIRST
boil 4L water in kettle

GEAR
5L saucepan
3L saucepan
chopping board
knife
fine grater
wooden spoon
large mixing bowl
slotted spoon
colander
tongs

FOOD
4L boiling water
2 tsp fine salt
500ml vegetable oil
800g spinach and ricotta ravioli (8 minute)
¼ cup capers
6 cloves garlic
½ bunch flat-leaf parsley
2 lemons
½ bunch oregano
¼ cup avocado oil
½ tsp ground cumin
¼ tsp ground nutmeg
salt and pepper

10 Set the 5L saucepan over a high heat then add the boiling water and fine salt. Pour the vegetable oil into the 3L saucepan and set over a high heat.

9 Put the ravioli in the boiling water. Drain the capers and pat dry with absorbent paper. Peel the garlic.

8 Pick the parsley leaves. Cut the garlic cloves into quarters.

7 Finely grate the lemon zest into the large mixing bowl then halve the lemons and squeeze in the juice.

6 Stir the ravioli. Chop the oregano finely and add to the lemon. Fry the capers for 30 seconds until browned then scoop out with the slotted spoon and drain on absorbent paper.

5 Place the garlic quarters in the hot oil.

4 Remove the garlic from the oil with the slotted spoon and drain on absorbent paper. Put the parsley leaves in the hot oil and fry for 30 seconds then add to the garlic.

3 Drain the ravioli well in the colander then add to the large mixing bowl. Pour the avocado oil on top and mix well.

2 Toss in the spices and season with salt and pepper.

1 Stir in the fried capers, garlic and parsley then divide among four plates.

> Keep an eye on the oil temperature. You want it to be hot, but not too hot. A good way to test it is to drop a parsley leaf in. It should sizzle on contact, but not produce smoke.

PUMPKIN RAVIOLI
WITH SPINACH AND MASCARPONE

FIRST
boil 4L water in kettle

GEAR
5L saucepan
chopping board
knife
frying pan
wooden spoon
tongs
blender
colander

FOOD
4L boiling water
2 tsp fine salt
2 eschalots
1 clove garlic
1 green chilli
2 Tbsp unsalted butter
3 bunches English spinach
1 bunch flat-leaf parsley
600g pumpkin ravioli (8 minute)
1 cup white wine
300ml thickened cream
75g grated Parmesan cheese
salt and white pepper
½ bunch opal basil
200g mascarpone
2 tsp truffle oil (optional)

10 Set the 5L saucepan over a high heat then add the boiling water and fine salt. Peel the eschalots and slice finely. Set the frying pan over a high heat.

9 Peel the garlic and slice finely. Chop the chilli finely. Place the eschalots, garlic, chilli and unsalted butter in the frying pan and stir well.

8 Pick the spinach and parsley leaves and set aside. Add the ravioli to the boiling water and stir well.

7 Stir the eschalot mixture.

6 Pour the white wine into the frying pan.

5 Add the cream, Parmesan, spinach and parsley to the frying pan then season with salt and white pepper.

4 Pick the opal basil leaves and set aside. Stir the ravioli.

3 Pour the spinach mixture into a blender and puree until smooth.

2 Adjust the seasoning of the sauce as needed.

1 Drain the ravioli in the colander then return to the saucepan. Pour in the spinach sauce then divide among four plates. Add dollops of mascarpone, some drops of truffle oil (if using) and garnish with opal basil leaves.

'AGLIO E OLIO': ANGEL HAIR PASTA WITH GARLIC AND OLIVE OIL

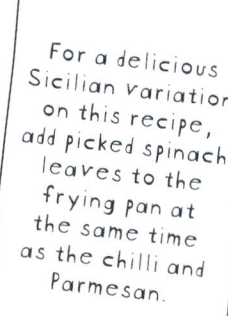

For a delicious Sicilian variation on this recipe, add picked spinach leaves to the frying pan at the same time as the chilli and Parmesan.

FIRST
boil 4L water in kettle

GEAR
5L saucepan
chopping board
knife
large frying pan
fine grater
wooden spoon
tongs
large mixing bowl

FOOD
4L boiling water
2 tsp fine salt
6 cloves garlic
6 anchovy fillets
2 lemons
1 bunch flat-leaf parsley
800g dried angel hair pasta
    (4 minute)
¼ cup extra virgin olive oil
1 cup breadcrumbs
1 red chilli
½ cup grated Parmesan cheese
salt and pepper

10 Set the 5L saucepan over a high heat then add the boiling water and fine salt.

9 Peel the garlic and chop very finely.

8 Chop the anchovies very finely.

7 Set the frying pan over a medium heat. Grate the lemon zest finely, then halve the lemons.

6 Chop the parsley finely. Drop the angel hair pasta in the boiling water, stir well.

5 Pour the olive oil into the frying pan and add the garlic, anchovies and lemon zest. Stir well.

4 Add the breadcrumbs to the frying pan and mix well.

3 Slice the chilli very finely.

2 Drain the pasta thoroughly and toss into the frying pan.

1 Stir in the chilli, Parmesan and parsley. Squeeze the lemon juice in, and season with salt and pepper. Mix well then divide among four plates.

SPAGHETTINI WITH ANCHOVIES, GREEN OLIVES AND ALMONDS

FIRST
boil 4L water in kettle

GEAR
5L saucepan
large frying pan
box grater
chopping board
knife
colander

FOOD
4L boiling water
2 tsp fine salt
2 Tbsp extra virgin olive oil
6 anchovies
1 lemon
2 cloves garlic
500g spaghettini (7 minute)
½ cup pitted green olives
¼ cup almond kernels
½ bunch flat-leaf parsley
¼ bunch mint
100g pecorino cheese

10 Set the 5L saucepan over a high heat then add the boiling water and fine salt. Set the large frying pan over a high heat.

9 Pour the olive oil into the frying pan and add the anchovies. Finely grate the zest of the lemon into the frying pan. Peel the garlic.

8 Slice the garlic finely and stir in with the anchovies. Reduce the heat to medium. Place the spaghettini in the boiling water.

7 Chop the olives roughly and stir into the frying pan.

6 Crush the almonds and add to the frying pan. Peel the lemon.

5 Stir the spaghettini. Chop the parsley very finely.

4 Stir the frying pan. Chop the mint very finely.

3 Dice the lemon flesh and mix in with the olives.

2 Grate the pecorino.

1 Drain the pasta well in the colander then stir into the frying pan with the chopped herbs and pecorino. Divide among four plates.

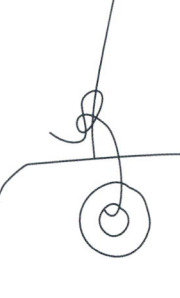

Cooking time varies from brand to brand of pasta. I have allowed 7 minutes, which is pretty common, but take a look at the instructions on the packet.

SPAGHETTINI WITH CHICKEN, MUSHROOM AND TARRAGON RAGU

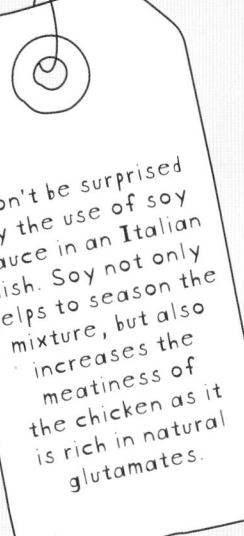

Don't be surprised by the use of soy sauce in an Italian dish. Soy not only helps to season the mixture, but also increases the meatiness of the chicken as it is rich in natural glutamates.

FIRST
boil 4L water in kettle

GEAR
5L saucepan
3L saucepan
chopping board
knife
wooden spoon
food processor
colander
tongs
vegetable peeler

FOOD
4L boiling water
2 tsp fine salt
2 cloves garlic
2 Tbsp extra virgin olive oil
500g chicken mince
200g button mushrooms
2 spring onions
500g dried spaghettini (7 minute)
1 bunch tarragon
salt and pepper
1 tsp dried Italian herbs
2 tsp soy sauce
¼ cup thickened cream
100g Taleggio cheese
80g Parmesan cheese
½ tsp ground nutmeg

10 Set the 5L saucepan over a high heat then add the boiling water and fine salt. Set the 3L saucepan over a high heat. Peel the garlic and chop finely.

9 Pour the olive oil into the 3L saucepan then add the chicken mince and break up using a wooden spoon. Place the mushrooms in the food processor and pulse several times to break up into small pieces.

8 Chop the white part of the spring onions finely, reserving the green section. Stir the chicken mince. Add the spaghettini to the boiling water and stir well.

7 Pick the tarragon leaves and set aside. Add the spring onion and garlic to the chicken mince and stir thoroughly.

6 Stir the mushroms into the chicken mixture. Then season with salt and pepper and stir in the dried Italian herbs.

5 Stir the spaghettini. Stir the chicken mixture.

4 Add the soy sauce and cream to the chicken mixture and stir well. Finely slice the green ends of the spring onions and set aside.

3 Mix the Taleggio into the chicken mixture. Shave the Parmesan into long strips using a vegetable peeler.

2 Mix the nutmeg into the chicken ragu.

1 Drain the spaghettini in the colander and stir into the chicken ragu. Mix in the tarragon and spring onion greens. Divide among four plates and garnish with shaved Parmesan.

SPAGHETTINI IN ROCKET PESTO WITH SMOKED TROUT AND WALNUTS

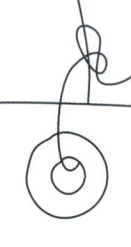

There's a big difference between rocket (the rounded flat leaf plant) and rucola (the spiky small leaf plant). Rucola is sometimes sold as 'baby rocket' but this is inaccurate. Use rocket for this recipe for its peppery flavour and delicate texture.

FIRST
boil 4L water in kettle

GEAR
5L saucepan
food processor
chopping board
knife
colander
large mixing bowl

FOOD
4L boiling water
2 tsp fine salt
1 bunch rocket
½ bunch basil
500g spaghettini (7 minute)
1 clove garlic
¼ cup pine nuts
¼ cup grated Parmesan cheese
½ cup extra virgin olive oil
1 tsp white wine vinegar
salt and pepper
1 smoked trout
½ bunch dill
½ cup walnuts
1 long red chilli

10 Set the 5L saucepan on a high heat then add the boiling water and fine salt. Tear the rocket leaves and place in the food processor.

9 Pick the basil leaves and add to the rocket. Add the spaghettini to the boiling water and stir well.

8 Peel the garlic and crush lightly then add to the food processor.

7 Add the pine nuts, Parmesan, olive oil and vinegar to the food processor and puree until it forms a smooth paste. Season with salt and pepper.

6 Stir the spaghettini. Peel the smoked trout.

5 Gently prise the trout flesh off the bones and break up into small pieces watching out for small bones.

4 Pick the dill sprigs and chop the walnuts.

3 Chop the long red chilli finely.

2 Drain the pasta well in the colander then add to the large mixing bowl. Toss in the rocket pesto.

1 Mix the trout, dill, walnuts and chilli with the pasta then divide among four plates.

LIGHT SPEED MINESTRONE

FIRST
set the 5L saucepan on high heat
warm 4 serving bowls

GEAR
5L saucepan
chopping board
knife
colander
vegetable peeler
wooden spoon
ladle

FOOD
1 leek
1 carrot
2 sticks celery
2 Tbsp extra virgin olive oil
2 cloves garlic
½ bunch thyme
salt and pepper
1L liquid vegetable stock
400g whole peeled tomatoes
250g dried angel hair pasta
   (4 minute)
¼ bunch sage
½ bunch basil
½ cup grated Parmesan cheese
1 tsp brown sugar

10 Dice the leek finely and rinse well in the colander.

9 Peel the carrot and dice finely. Chop the celery into small pieces. Pour the olive oil into the hot saucepan and add the chopped vegetables.

8 Peel the garlic and slice finely. Chop the thyme finely. Stir the vegetables.

7 Add the garlic and thyme to the saucepan and stir well. Season generously with salt and pepper.

6 Add the vegetable stock to the saucepan. Break up the whole peeled tomatoes roughly with a knife and add to the saucepan.

5 Snap the pasta into small pieces and add to the saucepan.

4 Stir well.

3 Pick the sage and basil leaves and tear into small pieces.

2 Stir the Parmesan and sugar into the soup and check the seasoning.

1 Stir in the herbs and ladle the minestrone among the warmed bowls.

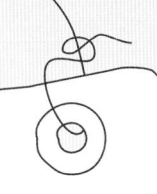

Boil some cotechino sausage and slice into small pieces then add to the soup for an elegant meaty version.

GNOCCHI IN THREE CHEESES WITH THYME AND PINE NUTS

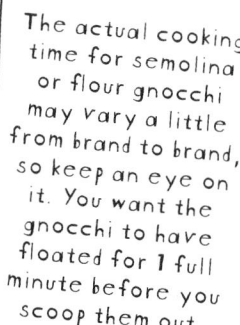

The actual cooking time for semolina or flour gnocchi may vary a little from brand to brand, so keep an eye on it. You want the gnocchi to have floated for 1 full minute before you scoop them out.

FIRST
boil 4L water in kettle

GEAR
5L saucepan
large frying pan
chopping board
knife
wooden spoon
box grater
slotted spoon

FOOD
4L boiling water
2 tsp fine salt
1 brown onion
2 cloves garlic
2 Tbsp extra virgin olive oil
salt and white pepper
2 green zucchini
½ cup liquid chicken stock
300ml thickened cream
800g semolina gnocchi
100g blue cheese
½ bunch thyme
80g Parmesan cheese
100g provolone cheese
1 tsp sherry vinegar
100g pine nuts

10 Set the 5L saucepan over a high heat then add the boiling water and fine salt. Peel the onion and garlic.

9 Set the large frying pan over a high heat. Finely dice the onion and mince the garlic.

8 Place the onion, garlic and olive oil in the frying pan and stir well. Season with salt and white pepper.

7 Dice the zucchini finely.

6 Stir the zucchini into the onion mixture.

5 Pour the chicken stock and cream into the frying pan and stir thoroughly. Add the gnocchi to the boiling water and stir.

4 Crumble the blue cheese into the frying pan. Pick the thyme leaves.

3 Shred the Parmesan on the coarse blade of a box grater, then transfer to the frying pan. Once the gnocchi are floating scoop out of the boiling water with a slotted spoon and transfer to the frying pan.

2 Shred the provolone on the coarse blade of a box grater, then transfer to the frying pan.

1 Stir in the thyme, sherry vinegar and pine nuts and adjust seasoning. Divide among four plates.

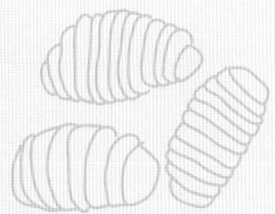

POTATO GNOCCHI IN A CREAMY CAPSICUM SAUCE

To roast your own capsicums, simply char them over an open flame until blackened then place in a bowl and wrap with cling film. When they cool, the skin will slip off and you can remove the seeds easily. Resist the temptation to rinse them as it washes away the flavour.

FIRST
boil 4L water in kettle

GEAR
5L saucepan
chopping board
knife
frying pan
wooden spoon
tongs
food processor
slotted spoon

FOOD
4L boiling water
2 tsp fine salt
1 red onion
1 clove garlic
1 Tbsp extra virgin olive oil
250g roasted capsicums
½ cup sweet sherry
1 vegetable stock cube
2 Tbsp tomato paste
2 Tbsp spicy tomato relish
600ml thickened cream
salt and white pepper
800g potato gnocchi
300g bocconcini cheese
¼ bunch lemon thyme

10 Set the 5L saucepan over a high heat then add the boiling water and fine salt. Peel the red onion and garlic. Set the frying pan over a high heat.

9 Finely dice the onion and garlic, then place in the frying pan with the olive oil. Stir well.

8 Carefully remove any skin or seeds from the capsicums then place in the food processor.

7 Add the sherry and vegetable stock cube to the frying pan and reduce the heat to medium.

6 Put the tomato paste, tomato relish and cream in the food processor and puree until it forms a smooth sauce.

5 Pour the capsicum cream into the frying pan. Season generously with salt and white pepper.

4 Add the gnocchi to the boiling water. Check the seasoning of the capsicum cream.

3 Cut the bocconcini into small pieces.

2 Pick the lemon thyme. As soon as the gnocchi float scoop them out of the saucepan with a slotted spoon and transfer to the frying pan.

1 Stir the bocconcini into the frying pan then divide among four plates. Sprinkle with lemon thyme leaves.

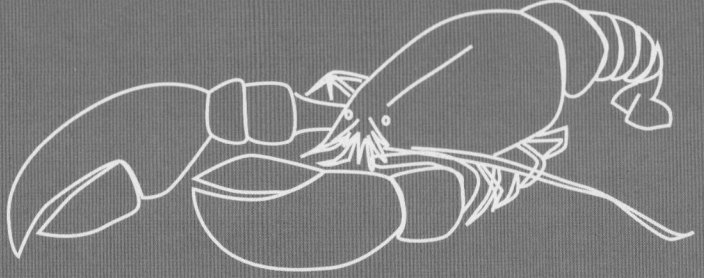

SHELLFISH

STEAMED OYSTERS IN LIME OIL WITH CRISPY FRIED NOODLES AND SHALLOTS

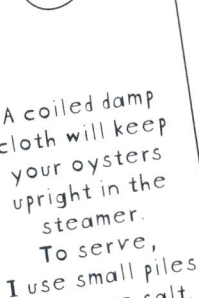

A coiled damp cloth will keep your oysters upright in the steamer. To serve, I use small piles of coarse salt.

FIRST
boil the kettle

GEAR
steamer
chopping board
knife
zester
mortar and pestle
small mixing bowl
frying pan
tongs

FOOD
24 shucked rock oysters
2 limes
1 eschalot
1 clove garlic
1 Tbsp extra virgin olive oil
2 tsp soy sauce
2 shallots
¼ cup miniature herbs
1 cup vegetable oil
50g rice vermicelli noodles

10 Set the steamer base over a medium heat and half-fill with boiling water. Arrange the oysters in a steamer basket, taking care not to spill their juices.

9 Zest the limes into the mortar. Peel the eschalot and garlic then chop roughly, then place in the mortar.

8 Pound the lime mixture until it is smooth, then stir in the olive oil and soy sauce. Spoon over the oysters.

7 Fit the steamer basket. Set the frying pan over a high heat.

6 Slice the shallots very finely and place in the small mixing bowl.

5 Pick the miniature herb leaves and add to the shallots.

4 Pour the vegetable oil into the hot frying pan.

3 Fry the rice vermicelli in the hot oil until it no longer bubbles, then drain on absorbent paper.

2 Crumble the noodles and add to the herb mixture. Cut the limes in half.

1 Arrange the oysters on four plates and top each one with a pile of the noodle mixture. Squeeze a little lime juice over the top.

SHELLFISH

VIETNAMESE MUSSELS IN TAMARIND AND LIME

FIRST
set the wok on high heat

GEAR
wok
chopping board
knife
wooden spoon
small mixing bowl

FOOD
2 Tbsp peanut oil
2kg cleaned and bearded mussels
2 sticks lemongrass
2 kaffir lime leaves
5cm piece ginger
2 cloves garlic
2 Tbsp tamarind paste
3 cups liquid fish stock
1 lime
2 red birdseye chillies
¼ cup fish sauce
1 Tbsp cornflour
½ cup sherry
½ bunch coriander
¼ bunch Vietnamese mint
1 Tbsp palm sugar
salt and pepper

10 Pour the peanut oil into the hot wok and add the mussels. Stir well.

9 Slice the white part of the lemongrass and the lime leaves finely and add to the wok.

8 Chop the ginger finely and add to the wok. Peel the garlic.

7 Mince the garlic cloves and stir into the mussels. Stir in the tamarind paste and the fish stock.

6 Halve the lime and squeeze the juice into the wok.

5 Slice the chillies finely and stir into the mussels. Add the fish sauce.

4 Combine the cornflour and sherry in the small mixing bowl. Pick the coriander and Vietnamese mint and set aside.

3 Pour the cornflour slurry into the wok and mix well.

2 Stir in the palm sugar and season with salt and pepper.

1 Fold in the herbs and divide among four bowls.

> Most Vietnamese ingredients have a good shelf life, so don't worry if you only cook Asian now and then. Keep in mind that fish sauce really needs to be kept in the fridge.

SHELLFISH

BELGIAN MUSSELS
IN A CREAMY BAY LEAF SAUCE

FIRST
warm 4 serving bowls

GEAR
5L saucepan
chopping board
knife
colander
wooden spoon

FOOD
1 leek
2 Tbsp butter
2 sticks celery
1 Tbsp plain flour
2kg cleaned and bearded mussels
4 fresh bay leaves
1 bunch flat-leaf parsley
¼ bunch thyme
500ml white wine
salt and pepper
½ cup double cream
80g gouda cheese
4 slices crusty bread

10 Set the 5L saucepan over a high heat. Slice the leek finely and place in a colander. Rinse well under cold water to remove any dirt.

9 Place the butter and leek in the saucepan and stir well. Slice the celery very finely and add to the saucepan.

8 Sprinkle the flour onto the leek mixture and stir thoroughly.

7 Add the mussels and bay leaves to the saucepan and place the lid on.

6 Chop the parsley very finely.

5 Chop the thyme very finely. Pour the white wine into the saucepan and season with salt and pepper.

4 Add the cream to the saucepan and mix well.

3 Chop the gouda into small pieces and stir into the mussels.

2 Stir in the herbs and adjust the seasoning if necessary.

1 Divide among the warmed bowls and top with a slice of crusty bread.

TUNISIAN CHERMOULA PRAWNS WITH CRUSHED KIDNEY BEAN SALAD

FIRST

set the ribbed griddle or BBQ grill on medium heat

GEAR

ribbed griddle or BBQ grill
chopping board
knife
small mixing bowl
wooden spoon
colander
2 large plates
large mixing bowl
tongs

FOOD

20 large king prawns
2 Tbsp vegetable oil
2 eschalots
1 clove garlic
¼ bunch coriander
¼ bunch flat-leaf parsley
3 tsp ground cumin
2 tsp sweet paprika
2 tsp turmeric
¼ tsp chilli flakes
2 Tbsp extra virgin olive oil
salt and pepper
2 x 400g cans red kidney beans
¼ cup mayonnaise
3 Tbsp tahini
2 lemons
¼ bunch mint

10 Use a large knife to slice the prawns lengthways from the underside and butterfly them open, leaving the back shell intact.

9 Drizzle the flesh side of the prawns with vegetable oil and set aside.

8 Peel the eschalots and garlic. Dice finely and place in the small mixing bowl.

7 Chop the herbs finely and add to the small mixing bowl.

6 Stir the spices and olive oil into the small mixing bowl then season with salt and pepper.

5 Place the prawns flesh-side down on the ribbed griddle.

4 Drain the kidney beans in the colander and rinse well. Pour onto a large plate, then crush using the second large plate. Transfer kidney beans to the large mixing bowl then stir in the mayonnaise and tahini.

3 Turn the prawns then top with the chermoula mixture.

2 Halve the lemons and squeeze the juice into the kidney beans. Chop the mint finely and stir in. Season with salt and pepper then divide among four plates.

1 Top each pile of kidney beans with five prawns.

SHELLFISH

CUTTLEFISH SALAD WITH GINGER, BEETROOT, ORANGE AND CHILLI

GEAR
wok
chopping board
knife
vegetable peeler
large mixing bowl
wooden spoon
mandoline slicer

FOOD
600g cleaned cuttlefish
1 large beetroot
2 oranges
¼ cup peanut oil
2 long red chillies
2 kaffir lime leaves
8cm piece ginger
2 heads witlof
1 bunch basil
2 Tbsp avocado oil
1 tsp sherry vinegar
1 tsp green Tabasco sauce
salt and pepper

10 Set the wok over a medium heat. Slice the cuttlefish into very fine strips.

9 Peel the beetroot.

8 Slice the beetroot into very fine strips using the mandoline slicer then place in the large mixing bowl.

7 Peel the oranges and cut the flesh into chunks.

6 Pour the peanut oil into the hot wok. Slice the chillies and lime leaves finely and add to the beetroot.

5 Add the cuttlefish to the hot wok and stir well.

4 Slice the ginger into fine strips and stir through the beetroot mixture.

3 Stir the cuttlefish then remove from the wok. Split the witlof leaves lengthways and mix into the beetroot mixture.

2 Pick the basil leaves and fold into the beetroot mixture, then add the cooked cuttlefish.

1 Pour the avocado oil, sherry vinegar and Tabasco over the beetroot mixture, then season with salt and pepper. Mix well and divide the salad among four plates.

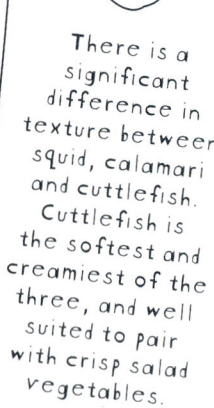

There is a significant difference in texture between squid, calamari and cuttlefish. Cuttlefish is the softest and creamiest of the three, and well suited to pair with crisp salad vegetables.

GOULD'S SQUID AND ASPARAGUS WITH FRESH FIGS AND WALNUT TARATOR

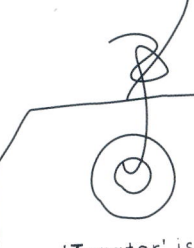

'Tarator' is a traditional Turkish sauce. It can be made with a range of nuts, but for seafood, walnuts are the best choice. Gould's squid are the small squid found in southern Australian waters. They are more tender and flavoursome than the arrow squid we import from New Zealand.

GEAR
wok
chopping board
knife
mortar and pestle
mandoline slicer

FOOD
600g small cleaned squid tubes
2 bunches thin asparagus
1 head baby fennel
100g walnuts
3 cloves garlic
2 slices sourdough bread
1 lemon
1 Tbsp white wine vinegar
125ml macadamia oil
salt and pepper
1 tomato
¼ bunch dill
¼ bunch parsley
2 Tbsp extra virgin olive oil
4 black figs

10 Set the wok over a medium heat. Slice the squid tubes into very fine strips.

9 Slice the asparagus in half lengthways and cut into 5cm pieces and set aside.

8 Shave the fennel finely on the mandoline slicer and set aside.

7 Place the walnuts and garlic in a mortar and pound to break up.

6 Slice the crusts off the bread and dice into small pieces. Add to the mortar and pound briefly.

5 Turn the heat under the wok to high. Halve the lemon and squeeze the juice into the mortar and pound until smooth. Stir in the vinegar and macadamia oil and season with salt and pepper.

4 Dice the tomato finely and set aside. Chop the herbs finely.

3 Pour the olive oil into the hot wok and add the sliced squid. Stir well.

2 Add the asparagus to the wok and toss well. Cut the figs into quarters.

1 Add the diced tomato, fennel and tarator sauce to the wok, then stir well. Gently fold in the fig pieces and divide among four plates.

SHELLFISH

SEARED SCALLOPS WITH SUN-DRIED TOMATO VINAIGRETTE, CREAMED CORN AND WATERCRESS

FIRST
turn on the grill

GEAR
large heavy-based frying pan
1L saucepan
knife
blender
large mixing bowl

FOOD
400g can creamed corn
1 orange
16 half-shell scallops
1 eschalot
2 Tbsp sun-dried tomatoes
1 gherkin
¼ cup extra virgin olive oil
2 tsp hummous
cooking oil spray
¼ bunch watercress
salt and pepper
½ head butter lettuce

10 Set the large heavy-based frying pan over a medium heat. Open the creamed corn then pour into the 1L saucepan and set over a medium heat.

9 Slice the orange in half and squeeze the juice into the creamed corn, then stir well. Remove the scallops from the shells.

8 Remove the adductor muscles from the scallops using a sharp knife. Pat the scallops dry with absorbent paper.

7 Peel the eschalot and chop roughly.

6 Place the sun-dried tomatoes, eschalot, gherkin, olive oil and hummous into the blender and puree until very smooth.

5 Turn the heat under the frying pan to high and spray with cooking oil.

4 Pick 16 sprigs of watercress. Place the scallop shells under the hot grill.

3 Arrange the scallops in the hot frying pan.

2 Pick the butter lettuce leaves and arrange as a base on four plates. Arrange four shells on each plate. Turn the scallops.

1 Place a spoon of creamed corn in each shell, then top with a scallop and season with salt and pepper. Spoon some sun-dried tomato vinaigrette over the scallops and top with a watercress sprig.

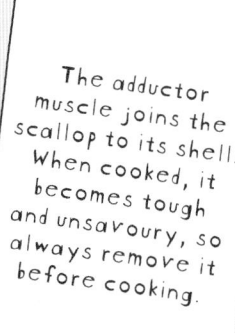

The adductor muscle joins the scallop to its shell. When cooked, it becomes tough and unsavoury, so always remove it before cooking.

BALCHAO: FIERY GOAN-STYLE PRAWNS

FIRST
set the wok on medium heat

GEAR
wok
chopping board
knife
wooden spoon
mortar and pestle
kitchen spoon

FOOD
2 brown onions
¼ cup vegetable oil
1.2kg peeled prawn cutlets
4 large tomatoes
2 cloves garlic
3cm piece ginger
2 red birdseye chillies
1 Tbsp ground cumin
1 Tbsp black mustard seeds
1 tsp ground cloves
1 tsp ground cinnamon
1 Tbsp brown sugar
¼ cup vinegar
½ bunch mint
salt and pepper

10 Peel the onions and dice very finely.

9 Pour the vegetable oil into the hot wok and add the prawns. Stir well.

8 Remove the prawns from the wok and set aside. Put the onions in the wok and stir well. Dice the tomatoes.

7 Peel the garlic and place in the mortar. Slice the ginger finely and add to the garlic. Stir the onions.

6 Slice the chillies and place in the mortar. Add the spices and sugar.

5 Add the tomatoes to the onions and mix thoroughly. Pound the spice mixture in the mortar until it forms a smooth paste.

4 Stir the vinegar into the spice mixture, then pour it into the wok.

3 Stir well. Chop the mint leaves finely and set aside.

2 Return the prawns to the wok and mix. Season with salt and pepper.

1 Divide the balchao among four plates and garnish with the chopped mint.

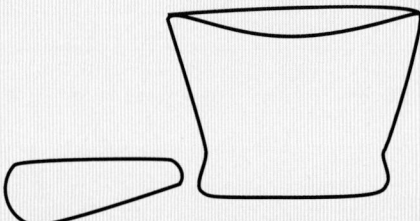

'YUM CHA' PIPIS IN XO SAUCE WITH ASIAN GREENS

FIRST
boil the kettle

GEAR
wok
chopping board
knife
vegetable peeler
box grater
wooden spoon
steamer
kitchen spoon

FOOD
5cm piece ginger
1 small turnip
2 Tbsp peanut oil
2kg pipis
¼ cup XO sauce
500ml liquid chicken stock
2 bunches choy sum
¼ bunch shallots
¼ bunch coriander
1 long red chilli
¼ bunch peanuts

10 Set the wok over a high heat. Slice the ginger very finely.

9 Peel the turnip and shred on the coarse blade of the box grater.

8 Pour the peanut oil into the hot wok and add the ginger and turnip. Stir well.

7 Add the pipis to the wok and mix thoroughly.

6 Stir the XO sauce into the pipis. Half-fill the steamer with boiling water and set over a high heat.

5 Pour the chicken stock into the wok and bring to a high simmer. Halve the choy sum lengthways and place in the steamer.

4 Slice the shallots very finely.

3 Pick the coriander leaves. Slice the chilli finely.

2 Crush the peanuts roughly. Remove the choy sum from the steamer and divide among four plates.

1 Spoon the pipis and wok sauce over the steamed greens, then garnish with shallots, chilli, coriander and peanuts.

Pipis are seasonal, so when they're not around, try this recipe with clams, vongole or mussels instead.

PESTO-GLAZED LOBSTER ON A ROUGH CAPONATA

Lobster isn't as expensive as you might think. Talk to your fishmonger about getting some smaller W.A. crayfish. They are affordable, and they taste great!

FIRST
turn on the grill to medium

GEAR
5L saucepan
chopping board
knife
baking tray
tongs
wooden spoon
colander

FOOD
2 x 1kg cooked lobsters
1 medium eggplant
1 brown onion
2 cloves garlic
¼ cup extra virgin olive oil
2 sticks celery
2 Tbsp capers
4 Tbsp butter
400g can whole peeled tomatoes
1 tsp brown sugar
1 Tbsp red wine vinegar
salt and pepper
¼ cup pesto
¼ bunch basil
2 Tbsp pine nuts

10 Set the 5L saucepan over a high heat. Split the lobsters lengthways, scrape out the alimentary canal. Place the lobsters on a baking tray shell-side up. Place under the hot grill.

9 Dice the eggplant into 1cm cubes. Peel the onion and garlic.

8 Pour the olive oil into the hot saucepan and add the eggplant. Slice the onion and garlic finely and add to the saucepan.

7 Slice the celery finely and stir into the saucepan.

6 Add the capers to the eggplant mixture. Turn the lobsters and smear with butter. Place the lobsters back under the grill.

5 Drain the tomatoes and add to the saucepan. Break up the tomatoes with the back of the spoon.

4 Stir the sugar and vinegar into the caponata, and season with salt and pepper.

3 Smear the lobsters with pesto and place back under the grill. Pick the basil leaves.

2 Stir the basil and pine nuts into the caponata and spoon in neat piles onto four plates.

1 Set a lobster half next to each pile of caponata.

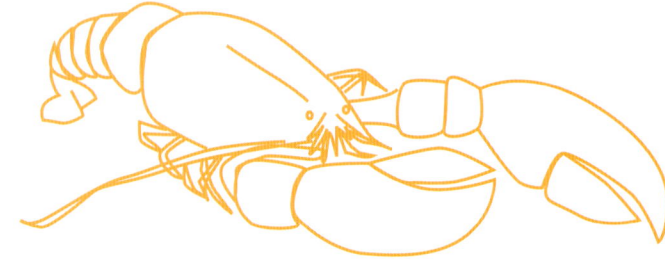

SHELLFISH

CRAB OMELETTE WITH WHITE ANCHOVIES AND RED ONIONS

GEAR
4 blini pans
large mixing bowl
whisk
chopping board
knife
mandoline slicer

FOOD
12 eggs
¼ bunch marjoram
2 Tbsp thickened cream
salt and pepper
4 tsp unsalted butter
1 red onion
1 bunch rocket
200g crab meat
¼ cup white anchovies
4 tsp green olive tapenade
½ head butter lettuce
¼ head radicchio
2 Tbsp extra virgin olive oil
1 Tbsp balsamic vinegar

10 Set the blini pans over a medium heat. Break the eggs into the large mixing bowl and whisk lightly.

9 Pick the marjoram leaves and add to the eggs. Whisk the cream into the egg mixture and season with salt and pepper.

8 Place a teaspoon of butter into each pan then divide the egg mixture among them.

7 Peel the onion and shave finely on the mandoline slicer.

6 Stir the egg mixture. Shred the rocket leaves finely.

5 Divide the onion and rocket among the four blini pans.

4 Arrange the crab meat, anchovies and tapenade on the omelettes.

3 Gently fold the omelettes over. Tear the lettuce and radicchio into bite-sized pieces and divide among four plates.

2 Turn the omelettes. Drizzle the lettuce with olive oil and balsamic vinegar, then season lightly with salt and pepper.

1 Place an omelette on each plate.

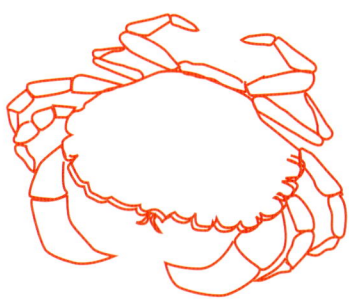

SHELLFISH

BARBECUED YABBIES IN PILSENER BASTE WITH COLESLAW

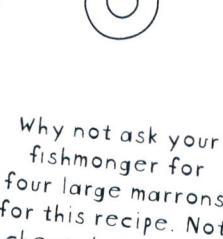

Why not ask your fishmonger for four large marrons for this recipe. Not cheap, but marron is the Rolls Royce of freshwater crayfish.

FIRST
set the ribbed griddle or BBQ grill on high heat

GEAR
ribbed griddle or BBQ grill
chopping board
knife
1L saucepan
large mixing bowl
tongs
small mixing bowl
whisk
pastry brush

FOOD
12 large red claw yabbies
2 Tbsp avocado oil
2 tsp celery salt
250ml Pilsener
2 Tbsp BBQ sauce
1 Tbsp golden syrup
¼ head red cabbage
¼ bunch dill
¼ tsp ground cardamom
salt and pepper
2 Tbsp Greek yoghurt
1 Tbsp mayonnaise
1 Tbsp horseradish cream
2 Tbsp currants
2 Tbsp pistachios

10 Split the yabbies lengthways. Drizzle with avocado oil and season with celery salt. Set aside.

9 Pour the Pilsener, BBQ sauce and golden syrup into the 1L saucepan and set over a high heat.

8 Shred the cabbage very finely and place in the large mixing bowl.

7 Pick the dill sprigs and combine with the cabbage. Sprinkle in the cardamom, season with salt and pepper, and toss well. Place the yabbies on the hot ribbed griddle flesh-side down.

6 Spoon the yoghurt, mayonnaise and horseradish cream into the small mixing bowl and whisk smooth. Add the currants and pistachios to the coleslaw.

5 Turn the yabbies. Add the yoghurt dressing to the coleslaw and mix well.

4 Baste the yabbies with the Pilsener mixture.

3 Baste the yabbies again.

2 Divide the coleslaw among four plates. Baste the yabbies again.

1 Place three yabbies on each plate.

SHELLFISH

FISH

TONNO TONNATO: GRILLED TUNA LOIN WITH TINNED TUNA MAYONNAISE

FIRST
set the ribbed griddle or BBQ grill on high heat

GEAR
ribbed griddle or BBQ grill
frying pan
tongs
chopping board
knife
small mixing bowl
food processor

FOOD
cooking oil spray
4 eggs
4 x 170g tuna steaks
salt and pepper
2 Tbsp avocado oil
2 sticks celery
1 red onion
2 lemons
185g can tuna in oil
1 tsp capers
¼ cup mayonnaise
4 anchovy fillets
2 bunches rocket
2 Tbsp extra virgin olive oil
1 Tbsp balsamic vinegar
½ bunch sage

10 Set the frying pan over a medium heat and spray with cooking oil. Crack the eggs into the frying pan.

9 Season the tuna steaks with salt and pepper, then drizzle with avocado oil. Place tuna steaks on the hot griddle.

8 Slice the celery sticks very finely and place in the small mixing bowl.

7 Peel the onion and slice as finely as possible. Add to the celery and mix well. Cut the lemons in half.

6 Turn the tuna steaks. Place the canned tuna, capers, mayonnaise and anchovies into the food processor and puree until smooth.

5 Squeeze the lemon juice into the tuna mayonnaise and pulse several times. Remove the eggs from the frying pan and scoop the yolks into the food processor and pulse a few times. Discard the egg whites. Season with salt and pepper.

4 Arrange the rocket leaves on four plates and drizzle with olive oil and balsamic vinegar.

3 Remove the tuna steaks from the griddle. Pick the sage leaves and stir in with the celery mixture.

2 Spread the tuna mayonnaise on four plates. Carve the tuna steaks into 2cm slices.

1 Arrange the carved tuna on the mayonnaise, then sprinkle the celery salad on top.

JOHN DORY IN YELLOW CURRY WITH WATER CHESTNUTS AND SNOW PEA SHOOTS

> John Dory is a spectacular flat fish with a moist, flavoursome and tender fillet. Unfortunately, it's very seasonal, and fairly pricey. A good substitute is Mirror Dory or flounder.

FIRST
warm 4 serving bowls

GEAR
large non-stick heavy-based frying pan
chopping board
knife
large mixing bowl
tongs
wooden spoon
vegetable peeler

FOOD
4 x 170g boneless John Dory fillets
1 Tbsp curry powder
2 Tbsp plain flour
salt and pepper
2 Tbsp ghee
2 cinnamon sticks
4 cloves
4 curry leaves
150g sweet potato
1 cup liquid chicken stock
2 Tbsp coconut cream
½ cup sliced water chestnuts
2 long red chillies
½ cup snow peas
½ cup snow pea shoots
½ bunch coriander
1 lime

10 Set the large frying pan over a high heat. Slice the fish fillets into large pieces and place in the large mixing bowl. Toss in the curry powder and plain flour, then season with salt and pepper.

9 Put the ghee in the hot frying pan then add the fish pieces.

8 Turn the fish pieces and add the cinnamon, cloves and curry leaves.

7 Peel the sweet potato and dice into ½-cm cubes. Add to the frying pan.

6 Pour the stock and coconut cream into the frying pan and stir well.

5 Turn the heat to medium. Add the water chestnuts.

4 Slice the chillies very finely and mix into the frying pan.

3 Top and tail the snow peas then slice finely. Add to the frying pan.

2 Halve the snow pea shoots then stir them into the curry. Pick the coriander leaves. Cut the lime into quarters.

1 Divide the curry among the warmed bowls and garnish with coriander leaves and lime wedges.

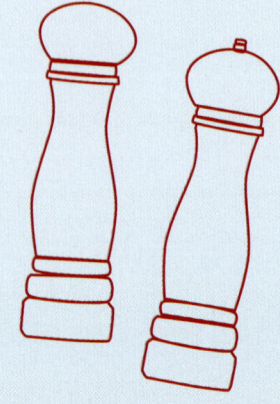

YELLOWFIN BREAM IN WHITE WINE AND HERBS WITH CHARGRILLED PUMPKIN AND TAHINI DRESSING

FIRST
set the ribbed griddle or BBQ grill on high heat

GEAR
ribbed griddle or BBQ grill
vegetable peeler
chopping board
knife
frying pan
tongs
2 small mixing bowls
whisk

FOOD
250g pumpkin
2 Tbsp mustard seed oil
salt and pepper
2 Tbsp plain flour
2 tsp cornflour
2 tsp celery salt
8 x 90g bream fillets
2 Tbsp unsalted butter
¼ bunch dill
¼ bunch thyme
¼ bunch parsley
1 Tbsp tahini
2 Tbsp extra virgin olive oil
1 tsp white wine vinegar
500ml white wine

10. Peel the pumpkin and scrape out the seeds, then slice the pumpkin in ½-cm pieces. Drizzle with mustard seed oil and sprinkle with salt and pepper then arrange on the hot griddle.

9. Set the frying pan over a high heat. Combine the flour, cornflour and celery salt in a small mixing bowl.

8. Coat the fish pieces in the flour mix. Add the butter to the hot frying pan and add the fish pieces.

7. Chop the herbs finely. Turn the pumpkin slices.

6. Turn the fish pieces.

5. Combine the tahini, olive oil and vinegar in the second small bowl and season with salt and pepper.

4. Add the white wine to the frying pan and shake well to coat the fish.

3. Add the herbs to the frying pan and adjust the seasoning.

2. Arrange the pumpkin slices on four plates and drizzle with tahini dressing.

1. Assemble the fish pieces on the pumpkin and spoon a little pan sauce over the top.

Go for a full fruit-flavoured white wine for cooking, but one with little or no timber notes. Chablis, Chenin Blanc and Riesling are my best picks.

BREADED SARDINE FILLETS WITH BEANS AND SALAMI

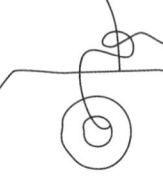

Sardines are baby pilchards. The best ones come from W.A., particularly around Fremantle.

GEAR
chopping board
knife
2 frying pans
2 small mixing bowls
whisk

FOOD
12 butterflied sardines
1 cup vegetable oil
8 slices hot Spanish salami
1 tsp extra virgin olive oil
1 red onion
2 cups green beans
2 cloves garlic
1 cup breadcrumbs
2 tsp dried Italian herbs
¼ cup grated Parmesan cheese
¼ cup walnuts
2 eggs
2 radishes
¼ bunch flat-leaf parsley
2 tsp cider vinegar

10 Check the sardines for any scales and remove these carefully with a knife. Pour the vegetable oil into a frying pan and set over a medium heat.

9 Slice the salami into very fine strips and place in the second frying pan with the olive oil. Set over a high heat and stir well.

8 Peel the onion and dice very finely. Set aside.

7 Top and tail the beans and set aside. Peel the garlic and mince it.

6 Stir the onion into the salami. Combine the breadcrumbs, dried herbs and Parmesan in a small mixing bowl.

5 Crush the walnuts lightly and stir into the salami. Crack the egg whites into the second small mixing bowl and whisk well. Discard the egg yolks. Turn the heat under the frying pan with vegetable oil to high.

4 Slice the radishes very finely. Add the beans and garlic to the salami mixture and season well with salt and pepper.

3 Dip the sardines into the beaten egg white, then into the breadcrumb mixture. Place the coated sardines in the hot vegetable oil.

2 Chop the parsley roughly then stir into the salami mixture with the radishes. Sprinkle with the vinegar, then divide among four plates.

1 Drain the sardines on absorbent paper then place three sardines on each plate.

GRILLED SWORDFISH WITH SPINACH, TOMATOES AND ARTICHOKE BUTTER

FIRST
set the ribbed griddle or BBQ grill on high heat

GEAR
ribbed griddle or BBQ grill
1L saucepan
food processor
frying pan
chopping board
knife
wooden spoon
tongs

FOOD
500ml liquid chicken stock
4 x 160g swordfish steaks
salt and pepper
2 Tbsp avocado oil
¼ cup marinated artichoke hearts
150g soft unsalted butter
4 spring onions
¼ bunch chives
1 oxheart tomato
   (or 2 vine-ripened tomatoes)
2 Tbsp extra virgin olive oil
2 bunches English spinach
1 Tbsp green olive tapenade

10 Pour the chicken stock into the 1L saucepan and set over a high heat. Season the swordfish steaks with salt and pepper then drizzle with avocado oil and set aside.

9 Place the artichoke hearts and butter in the food processor and puree until smooth. Set the frying pan over a high heat.

8 Slice the green stalks off the spring onions and discard. Cut the white bulbs in half and place in the simmering chicken stock. Turn the heat under the saucepan to medium.

7 Slice the chives finely and stir into the butter.

6 Arrange the swordfish steaks on the hot griddle. Roughly dice the oxheart tomato.

5 Pour the olive oil into the hot frying pan then add the diced tomato.

4 Pick the spinach leaves then add to the frying pan and stir well.

3 Turn the swordfish.

2 Season the tomato and spinach mixture with salt and pepper then stir in the tapenade. Divide among four plates.

1 Place a piece of swordfish on each plate and garnish with poached spring onions. Top with a spoon of artichoke butter.

SESAME-CRUSTED KINGFISH WITH FENNEL AND CUCUMBER IN ROAST CAPSICUM AGRODOLCE

GEAR
2 frying pans
chopping board
knife
tongs
vegetable peeler
teaspoon
wooden spoon
blender
small tray
colander

FOOD
4 x 170g boneless kingfish fillets
salt and pepper
2 Tbsp ghee
1 head baby fennel
2 Tbsp unsalted butter
1 Telegraph cucumber
½ cup verjuice
12 bocconcini cheese
¼ cup roasted red capsicum
2 Tbsp apple sauce
1 Tbsp caster sugar
2 tsp red wine vinegar
¼ bunch flat-leaf parsley
½ cup sesame seeds

10 Set a frying pan over a high heat. Season the kingfish fillets with salt and pepper. Place the ghee in the frying pan then arrange the kingfish in the pan.

9 Slice the fennel in ½-cm slices and place in the second frying pan with the butter. Set over a high heat.

8 Stir the fennel. Peel the cucumber and scoop out the seeds with a teaspoon. Slice on an angle 1cm thick.

7 Add the cucumber to the fennel and toss well.

6 Turn the kingfish and turn the heat down to medium.

5 Pour the verjuice into the fennel mixture and mix well. Baste the fish with its pan juices. Halve the bocconcini and set aside.

4 Put the capsicum, apple sauce, sugar and vinegar in the blender and puree until smooth. Season lightly with salt and pepper.

3 Chop the parsley very finely. Spread the sesame seeds on a small tray.

2 Drain the fennel and cucumber mixture in a colander then return to the frying pan and toss in the parsley and bocconcini. Place a spoon of capsicum agrodolce in the middle of four plates and top with the fennel and cucumber mixture.

1 Press each fish fillet onto the sesame seeds then place on top of the salad.

'Agrodolce' is Italian for 'sweet and sour' and is a style of sauce or dressing often used with seafood or game meats.

RAINBOW TROUT FILLETS WITH MISO AND CAULIFLOWER

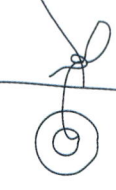

Bullshorn capsicums are long, sweet capsicums with few seeds. If they aren't in season, use a few long red chillies, but scrape out the seeds first.

FIRST
warm 4 serving bowls

GEAR
5L saucepan
chopping board
knife
food processor
vegetable peeler
wooden spoon
ladle

FOOD
2 brown onions
2 Tbsp vegetable oil
½ head cauliflower
4 cloves garlic
5cm piece ginger
2 Tbsp white miso paste
1L liquid chicken stock
8 x 90g boneless rainbow trout fillets
2 shallots
2 Tbsp soy sauce
1 red bullshorn capsicum
2 tsp black sesame seeds
1 tsp sesame oil

10 Set the 5L saucepan over a high heat. Peel the onions and slice finely.

9 Place the onions and vegetable oil into the hot saucepan and stir well. Peel any leaves off the cauliflower then break into large pieces.

8 Place the cauliflower pieces in the food processor and pulse until it forms coarse crumbs. Add to the onions and stir well. Peel the garlic and mince finely.

7 Slice the ginger into fine batons, then add the garlic and ginger to the saucepan. Stir in the miso paste.

6 Pour the stock into the saucepan and add the trout fillets. Put the lid on.

5 Slice the shallots finely and set aside.

4 Stir the fish stew.

3 Pour in the soy sauce.

2 Slice the capsicum into very fine strips.

1 Ladle the fish stew among the warmed bowls, then top with capsicum, shallots, black sesame seeds and sesame oil.

FISH

PROSCIUTTO-WRAPPED OCEAN TROUT WITH PRAWN TEMPURA

GEAR
frying pan
3L saucepan
chopping board
knife
tongs
2 small mixing bowls
large mixing bowl
whisk
slotted spoon

FOOD
1L vegetable oil
8 slices prosciutto
4 x 170g boneless ocean trout fillets
2 Tbsp ghee
½ cup plain flour
1 tsp dashi powder
¼ cup ice-cold tonic water
¼ cup ice cubes
½ bunch watercress
1 red birdseye chilli
¼ cup mayonnaise
2 Tbsp soy sauce
12 prawn cutlets
¼ cup rice flour
salt and pepper

10 Set the large frying pan over a high heat. Pour the vegetable oil into the 3L saucepan and set over a high heat. Lay four slices of prosciutto on a chopping board, then lay four more slices overlapping the first set to make four long strips.

9 Place a trout fillet on each strip of prosciutto and wrap well. Put the ghee and the wrapped trout fillet into the hot frying pan.

8 Put the plain flour and dashi powder into a small mixing bowl and stir well.

7 Pour the tonic water and ice cubes into the large mixing bowl, then slowly whisk in the flour mixture. Do not overwork.

6 Pick the watercress sprigs and set aside.

5 Turn the trout fillets and baste well. Chop the chilli finely and place in the second small mixing bowl.

4 Stir the mayonnaise and soy sauce into the chilli.

3 Baste the fish. Dip the prawns in the rice flour and then into the batter. Fry the prawns in the hot oil.

2 Arrange the watercress on four plates, and place a large dollop of soy mayonnaise next to it.

1 Drain the prawns on absorbent paper and season with salt and pepper. Place a trout fillet in the centre of each plate and top with three crisp prawns.

FISH

SALMON CUTLETS WITH A SIMPLE MORNAY SAUCE

GEAR
large frying pan
1L saucepan
3L saucepan
wooden spoon
whisk
chopping board
knife

FOOD
600ml milk
4 x 200g salmon cutlets
salt and pepper
2 Tbsp extra virgin olive oil
3 Tbsp unsalted butter
3 Tbsp plain flour
¼ tsp ground white pepper
½ tsp ground nutmeg
2 Tbsp brandy
¼ cup Gruyère cheese
½ cup breadcrumbs
2 tsp dried Herbes de Provence

10 Set the large frying pan over a high heat. Pour the milk into the 1L saucepan and set over a medium heat.

9 Season the salmon cutlets with salt and pepper then drizzle with olive oil. Arrange in the hot frying pan.

8 Place the butter and flour in the 3L saucepan and set over a medium heat. Stir well.

7 Add the white pepper and nutmeg to the butter mixture and stir.

6 Slowly pour the warmed milk into the 3L saucepan and whisk thoroughly.

5 Turn the salmon cutlets. Add the brandy to the sauce and whisk well.

4 Chop the Gruyère into small pieces and whisk into the sauce.

3 Turn the heat under the sauce to low and whisk thoroughly.

2 Add the breadcrumbs and dried herbs to the salmon pan and mix well.

1 Place a salmon cutlet on each plate. Drizzle with the mornay sauce, then top with the breadcrumbs.

Herbes de Provence is a southern French seasoning blend made from thyme, marjoram, lavender, basil, bay leaf and rosemary. You can get it pre-blended from good delis and spice dealers.

TANDOORI SALMON FILLET WITH CRUSHED CHICKPEAS AND CUCUMBER RAITA

Can't find paneer? Use a fresh mozzarella, like bocconcini or fior de latte.

FIRST
turn the oven on to 210°C

GEAR
2 small mixing bowls
baking tray
whisk
colander
2 large plates
large mixing bowl
chopping board
knife
box grater

FOOD
4 x 180g boneless salmon fillets
salt and pepper
2 Tbsp tikka masala paste
¼ cup coconut cream
2 x 400g cans chickpeas
2 limes
1 tsp garam masala
1 vine-ripened tomato
¼ cup paneer
¼ bunch coriander
2 Lebanese cucumbers
½ cup natural yoghurt
¼ bunch mint
½ tsp ground white pepper

10 Season the salmon fillets with salt and pepper. Mix the tikka masala paste and coconut cream in a small bowl then coat the fish. Arrange the fish on a baking tray and place in the hot oven.

9 Drain the chickpeas and rinse well in a colander.

8 Spread the chickpeas on a large plate, then use a second large plate to crush them. Transfer the chickpeas to a large mixing bowl. Cut the limes in half.

7 Squeeze the lime juice onto the chickpeas then add the garam masala.

6 Dice the tomato and paneer finely and stir into the chickpea mixture.

5 Chop the coriander finely and stir into the chickpea mixture, then season with salt and pepper.

4 Slice the cucumbers in half lengthways then scrape out the seeds. Shred on the coarse blade of a box grater into the second small mixing bowl.

3 Spoon the yoghurt into the cucumber. Chop the mint finely and add to the small mixing bowl. Stir in the white pepper then season with salt.

2 Make a platform of chickpea salad on each of four plates.

1 Take the salmon out of the oven and place one fillet on each plate. Top with a generous spoon of the cucumber raita.

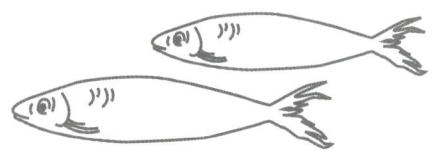

FISH

174

BARBECUED ALBACORE WITH EGGS, BEANS AND TOMATO

Albacore is a strong-flavoured member of the tuna family. It's always cheaper than yellowfin or bluefin tuna. The best comes from Queensland.

FIRST
set the ribbed griddle or BBQ grill on high heat
boil the kettle

GEAR
ribbed griddle or BBQ grill
1L saucepan
chopping board
knife
frying pan
wooden spoon

FOOD
4 x 160g albacore steaks
salt and pepper
2 Tbsp mustard seed oil
2 tsp white wine vinegar
2 cups green beans
4 eggs
2 cloves garlic
2 Tbsp extra virgin olive oil
2 punnets cherry tomatoes
½ cup pitted Kalamata olives
½ bunch basil
2 lemons

10 Season the albacore steaks with salt and pepper then drizzle with mustard seed oil and set aside.

9 Half-fill a 1L saucepan with boiling water and pour in the vinegar. Set over a medium heat.

8 Top and tail the beans. Set the frying pan over a high heat.

7 Break the eggs into the saucepan of boiling water and turn the heat to low.

6 Peel the garlic and slice finely. Arrange the albacore steaks on the hot griddle.

5 Pour the olive oil into the hot frying pan and add the beans.

4 Mix the tomatoes in with the beans and stir well.

3 Turn the albacore. Add the olives and garlic to the bean mixture and toss thoroughly. Pick the basil leaves.

2 Halve a lemon and squeeze the juice onto the beans and mix in the basil. Season with salt and pepper. Cut the other lemon into quarters.

1 Arrange the bean salad on four plates, then top with albacore steaks and garnish with lemon quarters.

DUKKAH-CRUSTED BLUE EYE TREVALLA WITH CARROT AND MINT SALAD

GEAR
large heavy-based frying pan
chopping board
knife
tongs
vegetable peeler
box grater
large mixing bowl
small tray

FOOD
4 x 180g boneless blue eye trevalla fillets
salt and pepper
2 Tbsp avocado oil
4 large carrots
1 Tbsp baby capers
¼ bunch mint
1 eschalot
2 lemons
2 Tbsp mustard seed oil
2 Tbsp butter
2 tsp cider vinegar
½ cup pistachio dukkah

10 Set the large heavy-based frying pan over a high heat. Pat the fish fillets dry with absorbent paper then score the skin with a sharp knife.

9 Season the fish with salt and pepper and drizzle with avocado oil. Arrange in the hot frying pan.

8 Peel the carrots, then shred on the coarse blade of a box grater.

7 Squeeze the excess moisture out of the grated carrot, then place into the large mixing bowl. Stir in the capers.

6 Chop the mint finely and add to the carrots.

5 Turn the fish fillets.

4 Peel the eschalot and dice very finely, then mix with the carrots.

3 Halve the lemons and squeeze the juice onto the salad. Dress the carrot salad with the mustard seed oil, season well with salt and pepper then mix thoroughly.

2 Turn the fish again and add the butter to the frying pan. Baste the fish several times. Drizzle with the vinegar. Pour the dukkah onto a small tray.

1 Divide the carrot salad among four plates. Dip each fish fillet in the dukkah then place a fillet of fish next to the carrot salad. Dress with some pan juices.

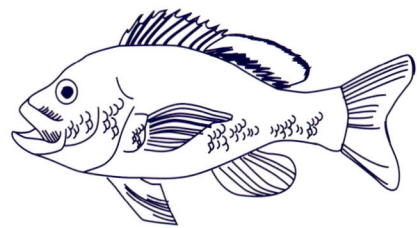

FISH

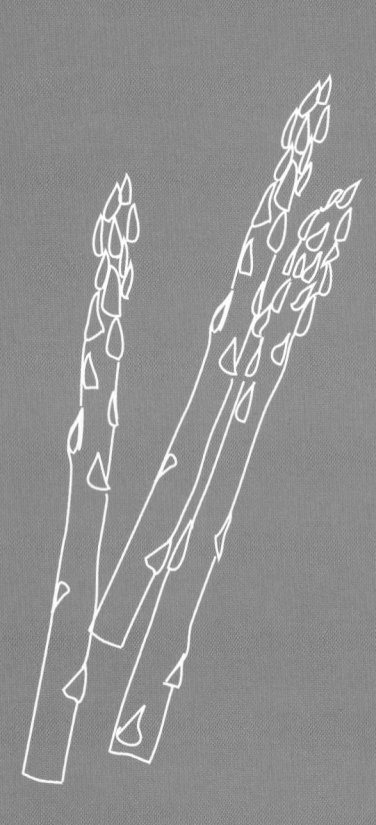

VEGETARIAN

FATTOUSH: LEVANTINE BREAD SALAD WITH TOMATOES AND HERBS

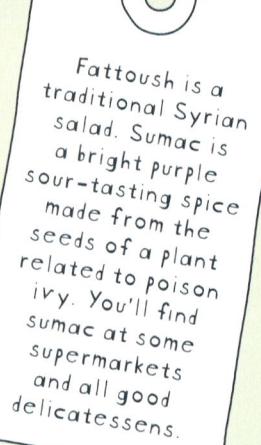

Fattoush is a traditional Syrian salad. Sumac is a bright purple sour-tasting spice made from the seeds of a plant related to poison ivy. You'll find sumac at some supermarkets and all good delicatessens.

FIRST
turn the sandwich press on

GEAR
sandwich press
chopping board
knife
large mixing bowl
vegetable peeler
tongs
wooden spoon
small mixing bowl
whisk

FOOD
2 Lebanese breads
2 Tbsp black olive tapenade
1 head baby cos lettuce
2 vine-ripened tomatoes
2 Lebanese cucumbers
4 shallots
1 green capsicum
½ bunch flat-leaf parsley
¼ bunch mint
1 bunch rocket
2 lemons
2 Tbsp extra virgin olive oil
1 tsp ground sumac
½ tsp hot paprika
salt and pepper

10 Cut the Lebanese breads open and spread with tapenade. Assemble them back together and place in the hot sandwich press.

9 Tear the cos lettuce into small pieces and place in the large mixing bowl.

8 Dice the tomatoes and add to the lettuce.

7 Use a vegetable peeler to shave the cucumbers into fine strips and mix into the salad. Chop the shallots finely and mix in.

6 Cut the green capsicum into very fine strips. Mix into the salad.

5 Finely chop the herbs and tear the rocket into small pieces. Add both to the salad.

4 Halve the lemons and squeeze the juice into the small mixing bowl.

3 Whisk the olive oil, sumac and paprika in with the lemon juice and season generously with salt and pepper.

2 Pour the lemon dressing over the salad and mix well. Remove the toasted Lebanese breads from the sandwich press.

1 Tear the breads into small pieces and mix into the salad. Divide among four plates.

VEGETARIAN

GARDENER'S FRITTATA WITH SPICY RELISH

FIRST
turn the oven on to 210°C
boil the kettle

GEAR
non-stick oven-proof frying pan
large mixing bowl
whisk
chopping board
knife
3L saucepan
vegetable peeler
box grater
wooden spoon
1L saucepan
colander

FOOD
12 eggs
2 Tbsp double cream
¼ bunch oregano
1 tsp truffle oil
salt and pepper
1 large carrot
1 zucchini
½ cup peas
4 pickled onions
1 vine-ripened tomato
¼ bunch thyme
2 Tbsp tomato paste
1 tsp honey
¼ cup feta cheese
¼ cup semi-dried tomatoes
¼ bunch parsley

10 Set the frying pan over a medium heat. Break the eggs into the large mixing bowl and whisk in the cream. Chop the oregano finely, whisk in the truffle oil, and season with salt and pepper.

9 Pour the egg mixture into the frying pan. Fill the 3L saucepan with boiling water and set over a high heat. Peel the carrot and grate coarsely.

8 Dice the zucchini finely, then place in the boiling water with the peas. Dice the pickled onions and the vine-ripened tomato.

7 Stir the egg mixture. Chop the thyme finely. Place the pickled onion, diced tomato, tomato paste, honey and thyme in a 1L saucepan and set over a high heat.

6 Stir the egg mixture lightly.

5 Drain the peas and zucchini in a colander then combine with the carrot and fold into the egg mixture.

4 Crumble the feta and arrange the semi-dried tomatoes on top of the frittata, then transfer into the oven.

3 Season the relish mixture with salt and pepper.

2 Chop the parsley finely and mix into the relish.

1 Remove the frittata from the oven and cut into wedges. Divide among four plates and top with relish.

VEGETARIAN

GRILLED FIELD MUSHROOMS WITH RICOTTA, PEAS AND MINT

FIRST
set the ribbed griddle or BBQ grill on high heat
boil the kettle

GEAR
ribbed griddle or BBQ grill
chopping board
knife
large mixing bowl
tongs
small mixing bowl
1L saucepan
food processor
zester
colander
wooden spoon

FOOD
8 large field mushrooms
¼ cup mustard seed oil
1 Tbsp Moroccan seasoning
1 cup peas
1 clove garlic
1 cup ricotta cheese
2 oranges
2 sprigs rosemary
salt and pepper
¼ cup almond kernels
¼ bunch mint
2 tsp balsamic glaze

10 Slice the stems off the mushrooms. Place the mushrooms in the large mixing bowl and toss in mustard seed oil and Moroccan seasoning. Arrange on the hot griddle.

9 Three-quarters fill the 1L saucepan with boiling water and set over a high heat.

8 Add the peas to the boiling water.

7 Peel the garlic and crush lightly.

6 Put the garlic and ricotta in a food processor.

5 Turn the mushrooms. Zest the oranges, adding the zest to the food processor. Halve the oranges and squeeze the juice into the food processor.

4 Finely chop the rosemary and add to the food processor. Puree until very smooth, then season with salt and pepper. Drain the peas in the colander.

3 Put the peas into the food processor and pulse several times. Chop the almonds roughly.

2 Chop the mint roughly and fold into the ricotta mixture. Remove the mushrooms from the griddle and top with the ricotta mixture.

1 Arrange the filled mushrooms on four plates, then sprinkle with almonds and balsamic glaze.

BLUE CHEESE POLENTA WITH EXTRAORDINARY MUSHROOMS

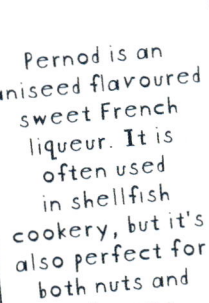

Pernod is an aniseed flavoured sweet French liqueur. It is often used in shellfish cookery, but it's also perfect for both nuts and mushrooms.

FIRST
boil 500ml water in kettle

GEAR
3L saucepan
wooden spoon
frying pan
tongs
chopping board
knife
vegetable peeler
large mixing bowl

FOOD
100g instant polenta
1 chicken stock cube
1 Tbsp unsalted butter
500ml boiling water
500g small Swiss brown mushrooms
2 Tbsp extra virgin olive oil
¼ cup skinned hazelnuts
1 turnip
1 red onion
1 bunch tarragon
80g blue cheese
2 Tbsp Pernod
¼ cup orange juice
½ punnet raspberries
salt and pepper

10 Pour the polenta into the 3L saucepan and add the stock cube and butter. Pour in the boiling water, stir well, and set over a medium heat.

9 Set the frying pan over a high heat and add the mushrooms and olive oil. Toss well.

8 Stir the polenta. Add the hazelnuts to the frying pan. Peel the turnip.

7 Dice the turnip and mix in with the mushrooms. Peel the onion.

6 Stir the polenta. Slice the onion into ½-cm-thick discs, then separate the individual rings.

5 Stir the mushroom mixture. Pick the tarragon leaves.

4 Stir the blue cheese into the polenta and season with salt and pepper. Pour the Pernod and orange juice into the frying pan and stir well.

3 Add the onion rings to the mushroom mixture.

2 Spoon the polenta onto four plates. Transfer the mushroom mixture to the large mixing bowl and stir in the tarragon, onion rings and raspberries. Season well with salt and pepper.

1 Assemble a pile of the mushroom mixture on each serve of polenta.

CRISPY KUMARA AND ASPARAGUS WITH PECORINO CRUMBS AND CAPER MAYONNAISE

GEAR

5L saucepan
vegetable peeler
chopping board
knife
large mixing bowl
box grater
small mixing bowl
food processor

FOOD

2L vegetable oil
4 bunches asparagus
500g kumara
1 cup ice-cold stout
1 cup plain flour
½ cup ice cubes
60g pecorino cheese
1 cup breadcrumbs
1 tsp dried thyme
2 eggs
2 cloves garlic
2 tsp mustard
2 Tbsp white wine vinegar
2 Tbsp capers
1 cup light olive oil
100ml white wine
1 cup rice flour
salt and pepper
½ head butter lettuce

10 Pour the vegetable oil into the 5L saucepan and set over a high heat. Trim the asparagus and peel the kumara.

9 Cut the kumara into ½ cm wide chips. Pour the stout into the large mixing bowl then stir in the plain flour. Gently stir in the ice cubes.

8 Shred the pecorino on the fine blade of a box grater then combine with the breadcrumbs and dried thyme in the small mixing bowl.

7 Separate the eggs and place the yolks in the food processor. Discard the egg white. Peel the garlic, crush lightly and add to the yolks.

6 Add the mustard, vinegar and capers to the food processor and puree until smooth.

5 Add the olive oil in a slow stream with the motor running. Drizzle the vegetables with white wine then coat in rice flour.

4 Dip the coated vegetables in batter, then in the breadcrumb mixture. Fry in the hot oil.

3 Season the caper mayonnaise with salt and pepper.

2 Divide the butter lettuce among four plates. Place a big spoon of caper mayonnaise on each plate.

1 Drain the fried vegetables on absorbent paper, season with salt and pepper. Arrange the fried vegetables in piles next to the mayonnaise.

Pecorino is a sheep's milk cheese traditionally made in Tuscany. It's a sheep's milk Parmesan. While the imported Italian varieties are the best available, there are some cracker local cheeses being made, particularly from some of our smaller artisan cheesemakers.

JAPANESE SOBA NOODLE SALAD WITH SESAME, SHALLOTS AND SOY

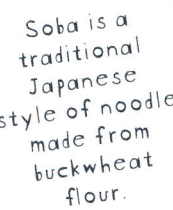

Soba is a traditional Japanese style of noodle made from buckwheat flour.

FIRST
boil 3L water in kettle

GEAR
5L saucepan
frying pan
small mixing bowl
wooden spoon
chopping board
knife
large mixing bowl
colander
tongs

FOOD
3L boiling water
2 chicken stock cubes
¼ cup white sesame seeds
2 Tbsp peanut oil
2 Tbsp soy sauce
2 tsp sesame oil
360g soba noodles
1 lime
6 shallots
2 Tbsp black sesame seeds
¼ bunch coriander

10 Pour the boiling water into the 5L saucepan and set over a high heat. Add the stock cubes and stir well.

9 Pour the white sesame seeds into the frying pan and set over a medium heat. Stir well.

8 Combine the peanut oil, soy sauce and sesame oil in the small mixing bowl.

7 Put the soba noodles in the simmering chicken stock.

6 Cut the lime in half and squeeze the juice into the soy mixture.

5 Stir the noodles. Remove the toasted sesame seeds from the frying pan and pour into the large mixing bowl.

4 Slice the shallots finely and add to the toasted sesame seeds. Stir in the black sesame seeds.

3 Pick the coriander leaves and mix with the shallots.

2 Drain the soba noodles in a colander and rinse under cold running water. Drain well.

1 Add the noodles to the large mixing bowl then pour over the dressing. Divide among four plates.

VEGETARIAN

EGGPLANT AND ONION PAKORAS WITH SOUR MANGO-COCONUT RELISH

GEAR
5L saucepan
chopping board
knife
mandoline slicer
2 large mixing bowls
whisk
large kitchen spoon
food processor
slotted spoon
tongs

FOOD
2L vegetable oil
4 Japanese eggplants
2 brown onions
½ cup chickpea flour (besan)
1 tsp ground turmeric
1 tsp garam masala
½ tsp chilli flakes
½ tsp ground coriander seeds
¾ cup ice-cold soda water
salt and pepper
1 mango
1 Tbsp tamarind paste
2 Tbsp coconut cream
1 Tbsp honey
2 eschalots
¼ bunch mint

10 Pour the vegetable oil into the 5L saucepan and set over a high heat. Slice the eggplants finely into bias-cut pieces.

9   Peel the onions and slice finely. Combine with the eggplant pieces and mix well.

8   Mix the chickpea flour and spices in a large mixing bowl, then slowly stir in the soda water. Season with salt and pepper.

7   Fold the sliced vegetables into the batter.

6   Cut the cheeks off the mango, scoop out the flesh with the large kitchen spoon, and put in the food processor. Add the tamarind paste, coconut cream and honey, and puree until smooth.

5   Drop large spoonfuls of the batter into the hot oil, ensuring that they do not stick together.

4   Peel the eschalots and dice very finely.

3   Pick the mint leaves and slice finely. Fold the eschalots and mint into the mango mixture.

2   Stir the pakoras.

1   Drain the pakoras on absorbent paper, then season with salt and pepper. Divide the pakoras among four plates. Place a spoon of the relish next to each pile.

STEAMED ZUCCHINI FLOWERS WITH ASIAGO AND PINE NUTS, CELERIAC REMOULADE

Asiago is a pungent cheese from Italy's northeast. It is available at most gourmet delis, but you can use Taleggio or Gruyère instead.

FIRST
boil the kettle

GEAR
steamer
frying pan
box grater
small mixing bowl
chopping board
knife
large mixing bowl
wooden spoon

FOOD
120g asiago cheese
100g ricotta cheese
2 Tbsp pine nuts
salt and pepper
12 zucchini flowers
1 head celeriac
2 Tbsp butter
1 apple
1 lemon
1 bunch chives
¼ cup mayonnaise
½ tsp hot mustard

10 Half-fill a steamer with boiling water and set over a high heat. Set the frying pan over a medium heat. Shred the asiago on the coarse blade of the box grater and place in the small mixing bowl.

9 Mix the ricotta and pine nuts into the asiago and season with salt and pepper.

8 Use a teaspoon to fill the zucchini flowers.

7 Peel the celeriac and shred on the coarse blade of the box grater. Put in the hot frying pan with the butter and stir well.

6 Put the filled zucchini flowers in the steamer.

5 Stir the celeriac. Shred the apple on the coarse blade of the box grater and put in the large mixing bowl. Cut the lemon in half and squeeze the juice over the top. Mix well.

4 Slice the chives finely and mix into the apple salad. Stir in the mayonnaise and mustard.

3 Mix the celeriac into the large bowl and season generously with salt and pepper.

2 Place a spoon of celeriac remoulade on each of four plates.

1 Arrange three filled zucchini flowers on top of each pile.

VEGETARIAN

ZUCCHINI, APRICOT AND MOZZARELLA ROLLS WITH BASIL AND SUNFLOWER SEED PISTOU

FIRST
turn the oven on to 220°C

GEAR
chopping board
knife
mandoline slicer
2 baking trays
small mixing bowl
food processor
tongs
wooden spoon

FOOD
4 large zucchini
salt and pepper
2 apricots
4 fior de latte mozzarella
2 Tbsp avocado oil
3 cloves garlic
2 Tbsp butter
1 tsp dried Italian herbs
½ baguette
1 bunch basil
¼ cup sunflower seeds
¼ cup extra virgin olive oil
¼ cup grated emmenthal cheese
1 tsp white wine vinegar
½ tsp icing sugar

10 Slice the zucchini finely lengthways and sprinkle with salt and pepper.

9 Split the apricots and place a ball of fior de latte on top of each apricot half.

8 Wrap the apricot sets in slices of zucchini and arrange upright on a lined baking tray. Drizzle with avocado oil and place in the hot oven.

7 Peel the garlic and mince one clove only. Combine in the small mixing bowl with the butter and Italian herbs.

6 Cut eight angled slices of baguette and smear with garlic butter then season with salt and pepper. Arrange the baguette on the second baking tray and set in the oven.

5 Pick the basil leaves and place in the food processor. Add the two remaining garlic cloves, sunflower seeds and olive oil to the food processor.

4 Puree the basil mixture until very smooth.

3 Fold the emmenthal, vinegar and icing sugar into the pistou, and season with salt and pepper.

2 Remove the baguette slices from the oven and arrange on four plates.

1 Put a zucchini roll on each plate and drizzle with pistou.

VEGETARIAN

LENTIL, OLIVE AND FETA STUFFED CAPSICUMS WITH THERMIDOR SAUCE

FIRST
turn the grill on to medium

GEAR
1L saucepan
colander
large mixing bowl
baking tray
5L saucepan
wooden spoon
whisk
small mixing bowl

FOOD
350ml milk
250ml sherry
8 roasted capsicums
400g can lentils
¼ cup pitted Kalamata olives
½ bunch marjoram
¼ cup feta cheese
2 Tbsp unsalted butter
2 Tbsp plain flour
¼ bunch flat leaf parsley
¼ bunch tarragon
2 eggs
2 Tbsp Dijon mustard
1 tsp Tabasco sauce
1 lemon
salt and pepper
¼ bunch watercress

10 Pour the milk and sherry into the 1L saucepan and set over a medium heat. Rinse the capsicums and remove any skin that may still be attached.

9 Drain the lentils in the colander and rinse under running water. Transfer to the large mixing bowl. Chop the olives roughly.

8 Set the 5L saucepan over a medium heat. Pick the marjoram leaves and stir into the lentils with the olives and feta. Spoon into the capsicums.

7 Arrange the filled capsicums on the baking tray and place under the grill. Put the butter and flour in the 5L saucepan and stir well.

6 Whisk the milk and sherry mixture into the 5L large saucepan, whisk well and turn the heat to low.

5 Chop the herbs finely and place in the small mixing bowl.

4 Separate the eggs and place the yolks in with the herbs. Discard the egg whites. Stir in the mustard and Tabasco. Halve the lemon and squeeze in the juice. Turn the grill to high.

3 Whisk the yolk mixture into the sauce, stir thoroughly, then season with salt and pepper. Turn the heat off.

2 Pour the sauce over the capsicums and place back under the grill. Pick the watercress into sprigs.

1 Place two capsicums on each of four plates and garnish with the watercress.

BEETROOT AND CORN 'RISOTTO' WITH SAGE AND SPINACH

GEAR
chopping board
knife
5L saucepan
vegetable peeler
box grater
vegetable juicer
wooden spoon
small mixing bowl

FOOD
6 ears corn
2 Tbsp unsalted butter
1 brown onion
2 cloves garlic
2 large beetroot
1 tsp capers
2 sticks celery
1 bunch English spinach
½ bunch sage
½ bunch flat-leaf parsley
250ml vegetable stock
salt and pepper
¼ cup marinated feta cheese

10 Cut the kernels off the corn. Put half the kernels in the 5L saucepan with the butter and set over a high heat. Reserve the remaining kernels.

9 Peel the onion and garlic and chop finely. Mix into the saucepan.

8 Peel the beetroots and shred on the coarse blade of a box grater. Add to the saucepan with the capers.

7 Pass the remaining corn kernels through a vegetable juicer. Pass the corn pulp through the juicer a second time.

6 Dice the celery sticks and stir into the saucepan.

5 Pick the spinach, sage and parsley leaves, then set aside

4 Mix the corn juice with the vegetable stock in the small bowl.

3 Pour the juice mixture into the saucepan and stir well. Turn the heat to medium and season with salt and pepper.

2 Stir the leaves into the 'risotto'.

1 Divide among four plates and top with crumbled feta.

CHARGRILLED ASPARAGUS WITH RICOTTA AND ARTICHOKES

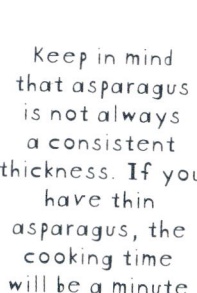

Keep in mind that asparagus is not always a consistent thickness. If you have thin asparagus, the cooking time will be a minute or so shorter.

FIRST
set the ribbed griddle or BBQ grill on high heat

GEAR
ribbed griddle or BBQ grill
chopping board
knife
blender
large mixing bowl
zester

FOOD
4 bunches asparagus
10 marinated artichoke hearts
2 Tbsp natural yoghurt
2 Tbsp extra virgin olive oil
2 eschalots
1 long red chilli
¼ bunch flat-leaf parsley
2 Tbsp mustard seed oil
2 lemons
1 gherkin
¼ head radicchio
salt and pepper
½ cup ricotta cheese

10 Trim the asparagus and set aside. Place two artichoke hearts, the yoghurt and the olive oil in the blender and puree until smooth.

9 Slice the remaining artichoke hearts finely, then place in the large mixing bowl.

8 Peel the eschalots and slice very finely. Add to the sliced artichokes.

7 Slice the chilli very finely and combine with the eschalots.

6 Chop the parsley finely, add to the salad, and mix thoroughly. Drizzle the asparagus with mustard seed oil and arrange on the hot griddle.

5 Zest the lemons, and finely dice the gherkin. Stir both into the salad.

4 Shred the radicchio and spread on four plates.

3 Season the salad with salt and pepper. Drizzle the artichoke dressing over the radicchio.

2 Arrange the asparagus spears on top of the dressed radicchio.

1 Sprinkle the salad on top of the asparagus, then crumble the ricotta on top.

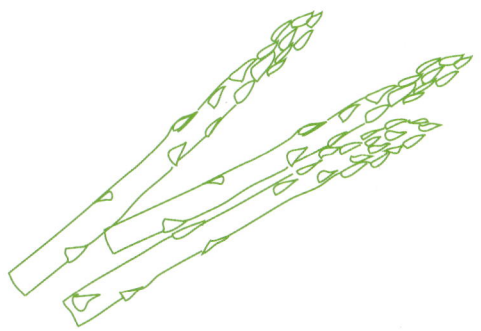

VEGETARIAN

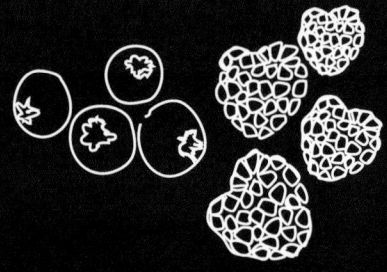

DESSERTS

RASPBERRY-RICOTTA TARTLETS WITH GRILLED PINEAPPLE AND LIME

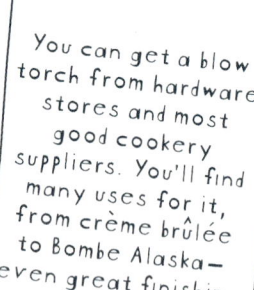

You can get a blow torch from hardware stores and most good cookery suppliers. You'll find many uses for it, from crème brûlée to Bombe Alaska — even great finishing touches to duck!

FIRST
turn the oven on to 210°C

GEAR
pastry brush
4 coffee cups
chopping board
knife
baking tray
large mixing bowl
whisk
small mixing bowl
wooden spoon
blow torch

FOOD
4 wheat tortillas
2 Tbsp macadamia oil
¼ pineapple
2 limes
500g ricotta cheese
100g icing sugar
½ cup caster sugar
2 punnets raspberries

10 Cut 15cm discs out of the tortillas and brush with macadamia oil on both sides.

9 Press the tortilla circles into four coffee cups and place in the oven.

8 Cut the skin off the pineapple and remove the core, then slice finely.

7 Arrange the pineapple in four 15cm discs on a baking tray.

6 Peel the limes and cut out the segments.

5 Put the ricotta and icing sugar in the large mixing bowl and whisk until smooth.

4 Sprinkle the pineapple discs with half the caster sugar then caramelise with a blow torch until dark brown. Remove the tortillas from the oven.

3 Sprinkle the remaining sugar on the pineapple and caramelise again. Place a pineapple disc on each of four plates. Garnish with lime segments.

2 Place a tortilla shell on each disc of pineapple and fill with the ricotta mixture.

1 Arrange the raspberries on the ricotta.

INSTANT MOCHA MOUSSE WITH ALMOND BISCUITS AND DESSERT WINE

GEAR
chopping board
knife
1L saucepan
electric mixer
small mixing bowl
spatula

FOOD
100g dark chocolate
100ml pouring cream
750ml thickened cream
100g pure icing sugar
2 Tbsp instant coffee powder
100g milk chocolate
200g amaretti biscuits
75ml sweet dessert wine
1 punnet raspberries

10 Chop the chocolate finely and place in the 1L saucepan. Add the pouring cream and set over a medium heat.

9 Stir the chocolate mixture. Pour the thickened cream, pure icing sugar and instant coffee powder into the bowl of an electric mixer and whip on medium speed.

8 With the cream at stiff peaks, turn the mixer off and transfer the cream mixture to the fridge to firm up.

7 Stir the chocolate mixture to ensure it is completely smooth.

6 Remove the chocolate mixture from the stove and drizzle on the inside of four chilled tall glasses, then return the glasses to the fridge to help the sauce set.

5 Chop the milk chocolate very finely.

4 Place the amaretti biscuits in the small mixing bowl and drizzle with the dessert wine.

3 Take the glasses out of the fridge and spoon a quarter of the cream mixture in the bottom, then top with some chopped chocolate and half the amaretti biscuits.

2 Spoon half the remaining cream mixture over the amaretti, sprinkle with chocolate and top with the remaining biscuits.

1 Spoon the rest of the cream mixture on top and sprinkle with chopped chocolate. Garnish with raspberries.

PEANUT BUTTER BROWNIE BALLS WITH SUGAR-CURED RHUBARB

GEAR
chopping board
knife
spatula
1L saucepan
small mixing bowl

FOOD
200g dark chocolate
100ml thickened cream
½ store-bought chocolate mud cake
¼ cup smooth peanut butter
4 sticks rhubarb
¼ cup caster sugar
½ cup peanuts
¼ bunch mint
2 Tbsp raspberry cordial

10 Chop the chocolate roughly and place in the 1L saucepan with the thickened cream and set over a medium heat.

9 Stir the chocolate mixture. Cut the cake into 1cm slices and smear each slice with peanut butter.

8 Stir the chocolate mixture. Slice the rhubarb as finely as possible and place in the small mixing bowl. Pour the caster sugar over the top.

7 Remove the chocolate mixture from the stove. Press the cake slices back together firmly, then cut into eight pieces. Squeeze each piece into a rough ball shape.

6 Chop the peanuts roughly.

5 Dip the cake pieces in the chocolate sauce, then roll in chopped peanuts. Place in the fridge to firm up.

4 Pick the mint leaves.

3 Stir the rhubarb.

2 Drizzle the rhubarb with raspberry cordial and mix well, then stir in the mint leaves.

1 Place two chocolate balls on each plate and garnish with a pile of the rhubarb salad and some of the syrup.

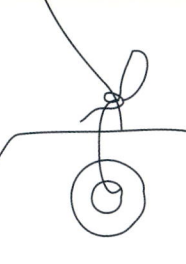

Rhubarb is fine to eat raw, and it has a lovely sweet-sour flavour. Buy the richest chocolate cake you can find, and refrigerate it ahead of time for best results.

FRIED FRUIT BREAD WITH BERRY-RIPPLED GREEK YOGHURT AND WAFERS

You want a good-quality fruit bread for this recipe. The supermarket stuff is OK, but not perfect. The heavier, the better.

FIRST
turn the sandwich press on

GEAR
sandwich press
large mixing bowl
whisk
chopping board
knife
small mixing bowl
wooden spoon

FOOD
2 eggs
100ml pouring cream
2 Tbsp icing sugar
1 tsp vanilla
4 thick slices heavy fruit bread
100g mixed berry jam
300ml Greek yoghurt
¼ cup caster sugar
8 chocolate wafer biscuits

10 Break the eggs into the large mixing bowl.

9 Whisk in the cream, icing sugar and vanilla.

8 Cut the crusts off the bread and dip the slices in the custard. Line a sandwich press with non-stick baking paper.

7 Arrange the bread slices in the sandwich press.

6 Spoon the jam into the small mixing bowl and stir thoroughly.

5 Add the yoghurt and fold gently to create a ripple effect.

4 Sprinkle both sides of the bread with caster sugar and cook again.

3 Slice the wafer biscuits into triangles.

2 Cut the fruit bread in half and arrange on four plates.

1 Spoon the yoghurt on top and garnish with wafer pieces.

DESSERTS

TRIPLE-STACKS OF SPICE BISCUITS, MANGO AND BRANDY CUSTARD WITH BLUEBERRY SALAD

GEAR
electric mixer
chopping board
knife
small mixing bowl
wooden spoon

FOOD
250g mascarpone
150ml custard
½ tsp brandy essence
1 mango
1 punnet blueberries
1 peach
1 kiwifruit
1 Tbsp orange liqueur
1 Tbsp icing sugar
12 Dutch Speculaas biscuits

10 Place the mascarpone, custard and brandy essence in the bowl of an electric mixer and whip on medium speed.

9 Once the custard mixture has reached stiff peaks turn the mixer off.

8 Slice the cheeks off the mango and scoop out the flesh.

7 Slice the mango finely.

6 Cut the blueberries in half and place in the small mixing bowl.

5 Cut the flesh off the peach and dice finely and combine with the blueberries.

4 Peel the kiwifruit and dice finely, then mix with the blueberries.

3 Drizzle the fruit salad with the orange liqueur and sprinkle with icing sugar. Mix well.

2 Lay a Speculaas biscuit on each of four plates and top with a spoon of custard, then lay some mango slices on. Set another biscuit on top, then custard, then mango.

1 Finish the stacks with a biscuit, then spoon the blueberry salad around.

'Speculaas' are a traditional Dutch spice biscuit with pictures of buildings on them. They are found in most supermarkets and good delicatessens.

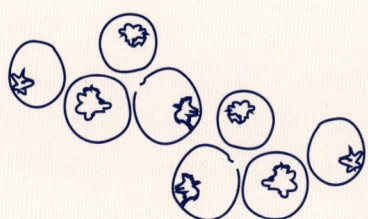

ROMAN STRAWBERRIES IN BALSAMIC, PEPPER AND MINT WITH HEAVY CREAM AND ORANGE SUGAR

GEAR
chopping board
knife
2 large mixing bowls
zester
mortar and pestle
whisk

FOOD
2 punnets strawberries
¼ cup pure icing sugar
1 tsp freshly ground black pepper
½ bunch mint
2 oranges
¼ cup caster sugar
300ml double cream
1 Tbsp good-quality balsamic vinegar
1 Tbsp amaretto liqueur

10 Cut the hulls off the strawberries.

9 Place the strawberries in the large mixing bowl and sprinkle with icing sugar and black pepper.

8 Pick the mint leaves and slice very finely.

7 Toss the mint through the strawberries.

6 Zest the oranges into the mortar.

5 Add the sugar to the mortar and pound until a smooth orange sugar forms.

4 Put half the orange sugar and the double cream in the second large mixing bowl.

3 Whisk the double cream to form stiff peaks. Sprinkle the strawberries with balsamic vinegar and amaretto liqueur and stir well.

2 Spread the strawberries and their sauce on four plates.

1 Put a large spoon of whipped cream in the centre, and sprinkle with the remaining orange sugar.

CARAMELISED FILO AND FIGS WITH STRAWBERRY SORBET AND IRON BARK HONEY

FIRST
turn the sandwich press on

GEAR
sandwich press
3L saucepan
chopping board
knife
pastry brush
ice cream scoop

FOOD
100g unsalted butter
4 figs
4 sheets filo pastry
½ cup iron bark honey
2 tsp mixed spice
½ cup caster sugar
½ cup thickened cream
¼ cup dark rum
1 cup strawberry sorbet

10 Put the butter in the 3L saucepan and set over a high heat to melt. Cut the figs into quarters and set aside.

9 Brush the filo sheets with butter, then pour the honey into the saucepan and return to a high heat.

8 Sprinkle the filo with mixed spice and caster sugar, then lay the sheets on top of one another.

7 Cut eight discs out of the pastry, line the sandwich press with non-stick baking paper, and arrange the pastry in the press.

6 Stir the honey mixture.

5 Stir the honey mixture.

4 Once the honey has caramelised, pour in the thickened cream and rum.

3 Stir the caramel sauce.

2 Scoop four large balls of strawberry sorbet and flatten slightly.

1 Place a disc of pastry on each plate then top with a disc of sorbet. Arrange the figs on top and finish with the final pieces of pastry. Spoon the sauce around.

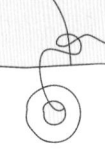

When figs aren't in season, this dessert works just as well with ripe pears.

APPLE FRITTERS IN CINNAMON SUGAR WITH WHITE CHOCOLATE SAUCE

GEAR
5L saucepan
large mixing bowl
whisk
box grater
1L saucepan
chopping board
knife
large kitchen spoon
slotted spoon
wooden spoon

FOOD
1L vegetable oil
1 cup self-raising flour
¼ cup icing sugar
¾ cup buttermilk
1 egg
2 Granny Smith apples
200g white chocolate
200ml pouring cream
1 tsp vanilla extract
2 tsp cinnamon sugar

10 Set the 5L saucepan over a high heat and pour in the vegetable oil.

9 Combine the flour and icing sugar in the large mixing bowl, pour in the buttermilk and crack in the egg.

8 Whisk the batter smooth. Shred the apples on the coarse blade of a box grater and fold into the batter.

7 Break the chocolate into pieces and place in the 1L saucepan with the cream and vanilla and set over a medium heat.

6 Stir the chocolate mixture.

5 Stir the chocolate mixture.

4 Place 12 spoonfuls of the apple batter into the hot oil, ensuring that they do not stick together.

3 Remove the white chocolate mixture from the stove.

2 Stir the apple fritters.

1 Drain the fritters on absorbent paper, then dredge in cinnamon sugar. Arrange on four plates and drizzle with the white chocolate sauce.

MELON SALAD WITH COCONUT SAUCE AND MANGO SORBET

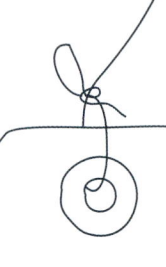

Make sure you use coconut cream, not coconut milk. It should be thick and white, almost solid, not runny. If you only have coconut milk, simmer the sauce for longer to reduce and thicken.

GEAR
3L saucepan
wooden spoon
melon baller
large mixing bowl
whisk
chopping board
knife
vegetable peeler
ice cream scoop
fine sieve

FOOD
½ cup caster sugar
150g rockmelon
150g honeydew melon
150g watermelon
1 cup pineapple juice
4 kaffir lime leaves
1 stick lemongrass
400ml coconut cream
¼ coconut
½ Madeira cake
1 cup mango sorbet

10 Pour the caster sugar into the 3L saucepan and set over a high heat. Scrape the seeds out of the melons.

9 Stir the sugar. Scoop the rockmelon using a melon baller and place in the large mixing bowl.

8 Stir the sugar. Scoop the honeydew melon using a melon baller and add to the rockmelon.

7 Stir the sugar. Scoop the watermelon using a melon baller and combine with the melons in the large mixing bowl.

6 Pour the pineapple juice into the sugar. Roughly slice the lime leaves and lemongrass and add to the juice.

5 Pour the coconut cream into the saucepan.

4 Prise the hard shell off the coconut, then shave strips of coconut flesh using a vegetable peeler. Combine the shaved coconut with the melons.

3 Cut four discs of Madeira cake and arrange these in the centre of four plates.

2 Spoon the melon salad around the cake.

1 Drizzle the coconut sauce through a fine sieve onto the fruits. Put a scoop of mango sorbet on top of each piece of cake.

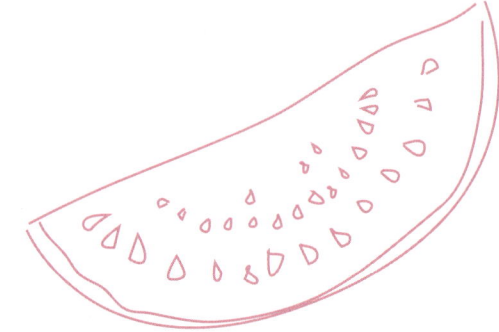

'KIND-OF-POACHED' APRICOTS WITH LYCHEES AND CARAMEL NUTS

FIRST
set the 5L saucepan on medium heat

GEAR
5L saucepan
wooden spoon
chopping board
knife

FOOD
1 cup caster sugar
2 cups dessert wine
1 vanilla bean
2 star anise
2 cinnamon sticks
2 kaffir lime leaves
12 apricots
16 lychees
100g peanut brittle

10 Turn the heat under the 5L saucepan to high and pour in the caster sugar. Stir well.

9 As soon as the sugar turns golden brown, pour in the dessert wine. Split the vanilla bean lengthways and add to the wine with the spices and lime leaves. Put the lid on.

8 Split the apricots and remove the seeds.

7 Turn the heat under the saucepan to medium and place the apricots in the liquid, put the lid back on.

6 Peel the lychees.

5 Cut the lychees in half.

4 Gently remove the lychee seeds. Turn the heat under the saucepan to low.

3 Chop the peanut brittle finely.

2 Take the lid off the saucepan.

1 Divide the apricots among four plates. Sprinkle the lychees among the apricot halves, then drizzle with the poaching liquid. Sprinkle peanut brittle over the top.

CHOCOLATE-HAZELNUT HOTCAKE WITH VANILLA ICE CREAM AND BLACKBERRY SAUCE

GEAR
frying pan
large mixing bowl
whisk
3L saucepan
chopping board
knife
wooden spoon
ice cream scoop

FOOD
2 eggs
¼ cup Nutella
2 Tbsp vegetable oil
½ cup natural yoghurt
½ cup icing sugar
1 cup self-raising flour
¼ cup hazelnuts
cooking oil spray
½ cup caster sugar
2 cup blackberries
2 Tbsp Frangelico liqueur
1 cup vanilla ice cream

10 Set the frying pan over a medium heat. Put the eggs, Nutella, vegetable oil and yoghurt in the large mixing bowl and whisk until smooth.

9 Set the 3L saucepan over a high heat. Whisk the icing sugar and flour into the egg mixture. Roughly chop the hazelnuts and fold in.

8 Spray the frying pan with cooking oil and pour in the batter.

7 Pour the caster sugar into the hot saucepan and stir well.

6 Stir the sugar. Give the frying pan a jiggle to ensure the hazelnuts are evenly distributed.

5 Add the blackberries and Frangelico to the caster sugar, stir well, and put the lid on. Turn the heat down to medium.

4 Gently turn the hotcake.

3 Give the frying pan a gentle shake.

2 Check that the hotcake is not sticking. Stir the blackberries.

1 Tun the hotcake onto a chopping board and cut into eight pieces. Place two slices on each of four plates, then spoon the hot blackberry sauce on top. Set a scoop of vanilla ice cream on top.

INSTANT CHOCOLATE CHEESECAKE WITH PISTACHIO-CRUSTED STRAWBERRY ICE CREAM

GEAR
electric mixer
spatula
box grater
chopping board
knife
baking tray
piping bag
ice cream scoop

FOOD
500g salt-reduced cream cheese
10g icing sugar
1 tsp vanilla extract
150g milk chocolate
1 pound cake
1 punnet blueberries
½ cup pistachio kernels
1 cup strawberry ice cream

10 Place the cream cheese, icing sugar and vanilla extract in the bowl of an electric mixer and beat on high speed.

9 Scrape down the sides of the bowl and beat until completely smooth.

8 Grate the chocolate on the coarse blade of a box grater and fold into the cream cheese mixture.

7 Cut four slices of pound cake and trim these into 10cm x 5cm rectangles. Arrange the cake on a baking tray.

6 Spoon the cream cheese mixture into the piping bag.

5 Pipe the cream cheese mixture onto the cake slices, then place in the freezer to firm up for a few minutes.

4 Halve the blueberries.

3 Chop the pistachios finely.

2 Make four scoops of strawberry ice cream then roll in the chopped pistachios.

1 Arrange the blueberries on each cake and place on four plates, garnish with a scoop of ice cream.

INDEX

aglio e olio 131
albacore, barbecued, with eggs, beans and tomato 175
almond biscuits with instant mocha mousse 204
anchovies and red onions, crab omelette with 155
anchovies, green olives and almonds, spaghettini with 132
angel hair pasta with garlic and olive oil 131
angel hair pasta with walnut sauce and ricotta 127
apple and chickpea salad, pork fillet and yabbies with 94
apple fritters in cinnamon sugar with white chocolate sauce 211
apples and dukkah, skirt steak with 77
apricot, zucchini and mozzarella rolls with basil and sunflower seed pistou 192
apricots, poached with lychees and caramel nuts 214
asparagus
    and beef rotoli with grilled radicchio 73
    and kumara with pecorino crumbs and caper mayonnaise 188
    chargrilled, with ricotta and artichokes 197
    salad, monte cristo with 40
    squid with fresh figs and 149
artichoke and gorgonzola toasts, spinach soup with 27
artichoke butter, grilled swordfish with 168
artichokes and ricotta, chargrilled asparagus with 197
avocado and lemon chicken quesadillas 116
avocado, tandoori 'lamb-burger' with hummous and 66

baby octopus with green curry and coconut with cucumber salad 47
bacon and leek omelette with cucumber and rhubarb salad 90
balchao: fiery Goan-style prawns 152
basil and sunflower seed pistou, zucchini, apricot and mozzarella rolls with 192
beef
    and asparagus rotoli with grilled radicchio 73
    bistecca alla florentina 72

chunky beef in tomato with crispy filo wafers 71
corned beef hash with grilled goats' cheese 81
Egyptian beef kofte 74
high-speed stroganoff 79
Irish steak and eggs 84
massaman-flavoured tournedos with lentils 78
peppered New York striploin steak with spicy tomato butter 75
scotch fillet with salsa verde and cavalo nero 83
skirt steak with salted apples and dukkah 77
Tuscan T-bone with lemon, olive oil and parsley 72
beetroot
    and corn risotto with sage and spinach 195
    and marinated feta tartlets with watercress 45
    borscht 22
    cuttlefish salad with ginger, beetroot, orange and chilli 148
    vermicelli with pancetta, beetroot and horseradish 124
Belgian mussels in creamy bay leaf sauce 145
bistecca alla florentina 72
blackberry sauce, chocolate-hazelnut hotcake with 215
blue cheese, lamb backstrap stuffed with, on tomato lentils 55
blue cheese polenta with extraordinary mushrooms 187
blueberry salad, spice biscuits with mango and brandy custard and 207
borscht on the run 22
bresaola, BBQ mushrooms with figs and 49
butter bean mash and tomato mayonnaise, pork sausages with 88

camembert, crumbed, with fennel and pine nut salad 36
caponata, pesto-glazed lobster on 154
capsicum
    agrodolce, sesame-crusted kingfish in 169
    lentil, olive and feta stuffed, with thermidor sauce 194
    potato gnocchi in creamy capsicum sauce 138
    soupy goulash of sausages and capsicums 24

caramelised filo and figs with strawberry sorbet 210
caramelised pears and onions, pork cutlets with 92
carrot and mint salad, dukkah-crusted blue-eye trevalla with 177
cauliflower and gorgonzola puree, five spice duck breast with 118
cauliflower, lamb neck fillet with cheesy fried 56
cauliflower, rainbow trout fillets with miso and 170
cavalo nero, scotch fillet with salsa verde and 83
celery potage with spicy sausage and prawns 30
celery salad, pork cutlets with cognac raspberry sauce and 101
chermoula prawns with crushed kidney bean salad 146
chicken
    and corn miso broth with scallops and almonds 16
    and sausage jambalaya 120
    and sourdough chargrilled skewers with chilli-lime baste 108
    BBQ chicken rice paper rolls with hoi sin and eschalots 113
    breast in riesling and cream with exotic mushrooms 111
    grilled thighs with radicchio, potatoes and sage 112
    larb gai: spicy Thai chicken salad 109
    lemon chicken and avocado quesadillas 116
    Moroccan-spiced spatchcock on couscous 115
    pesto-chicken coleslaw 41
    piri-piri drumettes with zucchini fritters and avocado 106
    smoked chicken pasta salad with walnuts and watercress 126
    smoked chicken, sweet potato and coconut gumbo 28
    soba noodle salad with ponzu dressing 117
    spaghettini with chicken, mushroom and tarragon ragu 133
chickpea and apple salad, pork fillet and yabbies with 94
chickpeas and cucumber raita, tandoori salmon fillet with 174

chickpeas and spinach, shiraz-basted backstrap with 61
chocolate cheesecake with pistachio-crusted
 strawberry ice cream 216
chocolate-hazelnut hotcake with ice cream and
 blackberry sauce 215
corn
 beetroot and corn risotto with sage and spinach 195
 chicken and corn miso broth with scallops and
  almonds 16
 fried lamb cutlets with Brussels sprouts and 54
 pistachio-crusted pork cutlets with grilled baby
  corn salad 102
corned beef hash with grilled goats' cheese 81
couscous, Moroccan-spiced spatchcock on 115
crab and cashew sang choi bao 42
crab omelette with white anchovies and red onions 155
cucumber and rhubarb salad, bacon and leek
 omelette with 90
cucumber raita, tandoori salmon fillet with 174
cucumber salad, baby octopus with green curry and 47
cuttlefish salad with ginger, beetroot, orange
 and chilli 148

dill crepes with tuna salad 46
duck, five spice, with cauliflower and gorgonzola
 puree 118
duck soup, hot and sour, with shallots and mint 21
dukkah-crusted blue-eye trevalla with carrot and
 mint salad 177
dukkah, skirt steak with salted apples and 77

eggplant and onion pakoras with sour mango-coconut
 relish 190
eggplant vindaloo, grilled chump chops with 64
Egyptian beef kofte 74

fattoush 182
fennel and cucumber, sesame-crusted kingfish with 169
fennel and pine nut salad, crumbed camembert with 36
feta and baby beetroot tartlets 45
feta, lentil and olive stuffed capsicums 194
feta, pork and fennel sausages with roman beans and 93

figs and bresaola, BBQ mushrooms with 49
figs and caramelised filo with strawberry sorbet 210
figs, Gould's squid and asparagus with 149
fish
 barbecued albacore with eggs, beans and tomato 175
 breaded sardine with beans and salami 166
 dill crepes with tuna salad 46
 dukkah-crusted blue-eye trevalla with carrot and
  mint salad 177
 grilled swordfish with artichoke butter 168
 grilled tuna loin with tinned tuna mayonnaise 162
 john dory in yellow curry 164
 prosciutto-wrapped ocean trout with prawn
  tempura 171
 rainbow trout fillets with miso and cauliflower 170
 salmon and pea fritters with redcurrant
  mayonnaise 37
 salmon cutlets with mornay sauce 172
 sesame-crusted kingfish in roast capsicum
  agrodolce 169
 smoked trout pâté with garlic toasts 44
 spaghettini in rocket pesto with smoked trout
  and walnuts 134
 tartare of kingfish with hazelnut romesco and
  fried lemon 38
 tonno tonnato 162
 yellowfin bream in white wine with pumpkin and
  tahini dressing 165
five spice duck breast with cauliflower and gorgonzola
 puree 118
frittata, gardener's, with spicy relish 184
fruit bread, fried, with berry-rippled greek yoghurt and
 wafers 206

gammon steaks with crisp herbed potatoes and Irish
 gravy 96
gardener's frittata with spicy relish 184
gazpacho for a summer day 29
ginger marmalade, sweet and sour pork in 100
gnocchi in three cheeses with thyme and pine nuts 137
gnocchi, potato, in creamy capsicum sauce 138
goats' cheese, corned beef hash with grilled 81

hazelnut-chocolate hotcake with vanilla ice cream
 and blackberry sauce 215
hazelnut romesco and fried lemon, tartare of
 kingfish with 38
hummous, tandoori 'lamb-burger' with avocado and 66

Irish steak and eggs 84

jambalaya, chicken and sausage 120
Japanese soba noodle salad with sesame, shallots
 and soy 189
john dory in yellow curry with water chestnuts and
 snow pea shoots 164

kidney bean salad, chermoula prawns with 146
kidney beans and snowpeas, oyster chowder with 25
kingfish, sesame-crusted, with fennel and cucumber
 in roast capsicum agrodolce 169
kingfish, tartare of, with hazelnut romesco and
 fried lemon 38
kumara and asparagus with pecorino crumbs and
 caper mayonnaise 188
kuybideh kabob 52

lamb
 and pancetta skewers with green bean and
  tomato sauté 59
 backstrap stuffed with blue cheese on creamy
  tomato lentils 55
 berber-spiced cutlets with classic waldorf salad 63
 'bit-over-a-minute' steak with mint spatzle and peas 58
 butterflied neck fillet with cheesy fried cauliflower 56
 chargrilled cutlets with parsley salsa and savoury
  french toast 60
 fried cutlets in wholegrain crumbs with Brussels
  sprouts and corn 54
 grilled chump chops with eggplant vindaloo 64
 kuybideh kabob 52
 shiraz-basted backstrap with chickpeas and spinach 61
 soy-glazed fillets with treacle on crushed
  white beans 65
 tandoori 'lamb-burger' with avocado and hummous 66

larb gai: spicy Thai chicken salad 109
lemon chicken and avocado quesadillas 116
lentil, olive and feta stuffed capsicums with
    thermidor sauce 194
lentils, creamy tomato, lamb backstrap stuffed with
    blue cheese on 55
lentils, massaman-flavoured tournedos with 78
lettuce and watercress soup with crispy onions 20
levantine bread salad with tomatoes and herbs 182
lobster, pesto-glazed, on caponata 154
lychees and caramel nuts, poached apricots with 214

mango and brandy custard, spice biscuits with 207
mango sorbet with melon salad and coconut sauce 212
massaman-flavoured tournedos with lentils, yoghurt
    and currants 78
meatballs with creamy tomato sauce and fried
    Italian bread 99
melon salad with coconut sauce and mango sorbet 212
minestrone, light speed 136
miso and cauliflower, rainbow trout fillets with 170
miso broth, chicken and corn, with scallops and almonds 16
mocha mousse with almond biscuits and dessert
    wine 204
monte cristo with asparagus salad 40
Moroccan-spiced spatchcock on couscous with
    oranges and lemons 115
mushrooms
    BBQ, with figs and bresaola 49
    blue cheese polenta with 187
    chicken breast in riesling and cream with 111
    grilled, with ricotta, peas and mint 185
    spaghettini with chicken, mushroom and
        tarragon ragu 133
mussels, Belgian, in creamy bay leaf sauce 145
mussels, Vietnamese, in tamarind and lime 144
neapolitan veal chops 82

noodles
    chicken soba noodle salad with ponzu dressing 117
    Japanese soba noodle salad with sesame, shallots
        and soy 189

pork loin chops in char siu sauce with crispy noodle
    salad 89
steamed oysters in lime oil with crispy fried noodles
    and shallots 143
wok-seared pork fillet with hokkien noodles and
    ginger 95

omelette, bacon and leek, with cucumber and rhubarb
    salad 90
omelette, crab, with white anchovies and red onions 155
onion and eggplant pakoras with sour mango-coconut
    relish 190
onions, crispy, lettuce and watercress soup with 20
onions, pork cutlets with caramelised pears and 92
oyster chowder with kidney beans and snowpeas 25
oysters, steamed, in lime oil with crispy fried noodles
    and shallots 143

pakoras, eggplant and onion, with sour mango-coconut
    relish 190
pancetta and lamb skewers with green bean and tomato
    sauté 59
pancetta, beetroot and horseradish, vermicelli with 124
parsley salsa and savoury french toast, chargrilled lamb
    cutlets with 60
parsnip soup, creamy, with wholewheat croutons
    and oregano relish 18
pasta
    aglio e olio 131
    angel hair pasta with garlic and olive oil 131
    angel hair pasta with walnut sauce and ricotta 127
    gnocchi in three cheeses with thyme and pine
        nuts 137
    minestrone 136
    potato gnocchi in creamy capsicum sauce 138
    pumpkin ravioli with spinach and mascarpone 129
    smoked chicken pasta salad with walnuts and
        watercress 126
    spaghettini in rocket pesto with smoked trout
        and walnuts 134
    spaghettini with anchovies, green olives and
        almonds 132

spaghettini with chicken, mushroom and tarragon
    ragu 133
spinach and ricotta ravioli with fried capers and
    garlic 128
vermicelli with pancetta, beetroot and horseradish 124
pea and ham soup (for vegetarians) 19
pea and salmon fritters with redcurrant mayonnaise 37
peanut butter brownie balls with sugar-cured rhubarb 205
pear, grilled, prosciutto sticks with 35
pear, prosciutto and basil salad, barbecued quails
    with 119
pears and onions, caramelised, pork cutlets with 92
peppered New York striploin steak with spicy tomato
    butter and peas 75
pesto-chicken coleslaw 41
pesto-glazed lobster on caponata 154
pine nut and fennel salad, crumbed camembert with 36
pine nuts, gnocchi in three cheeses with 137
pineapple, grilled, raspberry-ricotta tartlets with 202
pipis in xo sauce with asian greens 153
pistachio-crusted pork cutlets with grilled baby
    corn salad 102
polenta, blue cheese, with extraordinary mushrooms 187
pork
    and fennel sausages with roman beans and
        marinated feta 93
    chargrilled fillet and yabbies with apple and
        chickpea salad 94
    cutlets with caramelised pears and onions 92
    cutlets with cognac raspberry sauce and
        celery salad 101
    gammon steaks with crisp herbed potatoes and
        Irish gravy 96
    loin chops in char siu sauce with crispy noodle
        salad 89
    meatballs with creamy tomato sauce and fried
        Italian bread 99
    pistachio-crusted cutlets with grilled baby
        corn salad 102
    sausages with butter bean mash and tomato
        mayonnaise 88
    sweet and sour, in ginger marmalade 100

wok-seared fillet with hokkien noodles and ginger 95
potato gnocchi in creamy capsicum sauce 138
potatoes, crisp herbed, gammon steaks with 96
prawns
    balchao: fiery Goan-style 152
    potage of celery with spicy sausage and 30
    tempura, prosciutto-wrapped ocean trout with 171
    Tunisian chermoula prawns with crushed kidney bean salad 146
prosciutto sticks with grilled pear, honey and walnut salsa 35
prosciutto-wrapped ocean trout with prawn tempura 171
pumpkin, chargrilled, yellowfin bream with 165
pumpkin ravioli with spinach and mascarpone 129

quails, barbecued, with prosciutto, pear and basil salad 119
quesadillas, lemon chicken and avocado 116

radicchio, beef and asparagus rotoli with 73
radicchio, potatoes and sage, grilled chicken with 112
rainbow trout fillets with miso and cauliflower 170
raspberry-ricotta tartlets with grilled pineapple and lime 202
ravioli, pumpkin, with spinach and mascarpone 129
ravioli, spinach and ricotta, with fried capers and garlic 128
rice paper rolls, chicken, with hoi sin and eschalots 113
ricotta
    angel hair pasta with walnut sauce and 127
    chargrilled asparagus with artichokes and 197
    grilled field mushrooms with peas, mint and 185
    raspberry-ricotta tartlets with grilled pineapple and lime 202
    spinach and ricotta ravioli with fried capers and garlic 128
rocket pesto, spaghettini in, with smoked trout and walnuts 134
rhubarb, sugar-cured, with peanut butter brownie balls 205

salmon and pea fritters with redcurrant mayonnaise 37
salmon cutlets with mornay sauce 172
salmon, tandoori, with crushed chickpeas and cucumber raita 174
salsa verde and cavalo nero, scotch fillet with 83
sardine, breaded, with beans and salami 166
sausage
    chicken and sausage jambalaya 120
    pork sausages with butter bean mash and tomato mayonnaise 88
    potage of celery with spicy sausage and prawns 30
    soupy goulash of sausages and capsicums 24
scallops, chicken and corn miso broth with almonds and 16
scotch fillet with salsa verde and cavalo nero 83
smoked trout and walnuts, spaghettini in rocket pesto with 134
smoked trout pâté with garlic toasts 44
spatchcock, Moroccan-spiced, on couscous with oranges and lemons 115
spice biscuits, mango and brandy custard with blueberry salad 207
spinach
    and ricotta ravioli with fried capers and garlic 128
    beetroot and corn risotto with sage and 195
    grilled swordfish with tomatoes and 168
    pumpkin ravioli with mascarpone and 129
    shiraz-basted lamb backstrap with chickpeas and 61
    soup with artichoke and gorgonzola toasts 27
strawberries, roman, in balsamic, pepper and mint 209
strawberry ice cream, pistachio-crusted, with chocolate cheesecake 216
strawberry sorbet, caramelised filo and figs with 210
stroganoff, high-speed 79
sweet and sour pork in ginger marmalade 100
sweet potato, smoked chicken and coconut gumbo 28

tandoori 'lamb-burger' with avocado and hummous 66
tandoori salmon fillet with crushed chickpeas and cucumber raita 174
Thai chicken salad (larb gai) 109

tomato butter, peppered New York striploin steak with 75
tomato mayonnaise, pork sausages with butter bean mash and 88
tomato sauté, lamb and pancetta skewers with 59
tonno tonnato 162
tuna salad, dill crepes with 46
tuna, grilled, with tinned tuna mayonnaise 162
Tunisian chermoula prawns with crushed kidney bean salad 146

veal chops, neapolitan 82
vermicelli with pancetta, beetroot and horseradish 124
Vietnamese mussels in tamarind and lime 144

walnuts
    salsa, prosciutto sticks with grilled pear and 35
    sauce, angel hair pasta with 127
    smoked chicken pasta salad with watercress and 126
    spaghettini in rocket pesto with smoked trout and 134
    tarator, Gould's squid and asparagus with 149
    waldorf salad, berber-spiced cutlets with 63
watercress and lettuce soup with crispy onions 20
white chocolate sauce, apple fritters in cinnamon sugar with 211

yabbies, barbecued in pilsener baste, with coleslaw 156
yabbies, chargrilled pork fillet and, with apple and chickpea salad 94
yellowfin bream in white wine and herbs with pumpkin and tahini dressing 165
yoghurt, berry rippled, fried fruit bread with 206

zucchini, apricot and mozzarella rolls with basil and sunflower seed pistou 192
zucchini flowers, steamed, with asiago and pine nuts, celeriac remoulade 191
zucchini fritters and avocado, piri-piri chicken drumettes with 106

ACKNOWLEDGEMENTS

Books like this only happen when people from a range of disciplines decide to share their lunch boxes in the playground. So I really want to thank the following bunch of folks.

My thanks first to Jill Brown, my original publisher, for being a friend above all, because that matters most to me. But also for being a champion organiser, a keen director and, most of all, for being wonderfully straight-talking.

Chris Jones is the gold standard of photographers: artistic, technical, obsessed with detail. Not to mention he's a great guy to hang out with.

Yael Grinham, stylist, is a magician. From simple components of food she creates striking artworks rich with personality.

Jay Ryves designs beautiful books. She takes words and images, illustrations and dreams, then cooks them in her cauldron until a splendid book simmers to the surface. At least I think that's how the design process works.

Stephanie Kistner, editor, found the sense in what started out as a morass of words laid end on end. Editing is a seriously hard job, and she did it with finese. Oops, I mean 'finesse'. Sorry, Steph! Anouska Jones gave it all a sharp-eyed proofread and Susie Easton provided the detailed index. Thanks everyone for working so quickly and making the tight deadlines.

And at Random House, Joanna Penney, production controller, and Annabel Rijks, publicist, quietly get on with the important things a publishing house does to produce and then support a book. Most of which happens without my even noticing. Actually, it's a secret society; they have a clubhouse and everything.

My wife, Leah. Hmm. I was going to thank you for the beautiful illustrations you did and they are great. I was also going to thank you for the support you gave me in refining the concept of *Dinner in 10*. But really, it all comes down to a cup of tea at seven in the morning. You seem to know just the moment when all I need to get my fingers typing again is the sweet whiff of bergamot. No-one else does that.

Luca and Finn, thanks for giving me time to write, even if that did involve you sitting on my lap telling me about school most of the time.

And, finally, thanks to all the gang at *Better Homes and Gardens*, who always push me to create better and simpler ideas, and without whom this journey would never have gotten underway.

Ed

BIOGRAPHY

Ed Halmagyi is better known as Fast Ed, resident chef on TV's *Better Homes and Gardens*. His approach to cooking is liberating: keep it simple, because if you do less, the ingredients can do more.

After nearly 20 years cooking in restaurants around the world, including a stint at Sydney's iconic Rockpool, Ed now works as a media presenter, author and consultant. In addition to BH&G, he has hosted his own afternoon cooking show; the weekly BH&G radio show; and a travel series through Australia's south.

But at heart Ed is a secret gardener with a passion for growing heirloom vegetables in his beachside backyard.

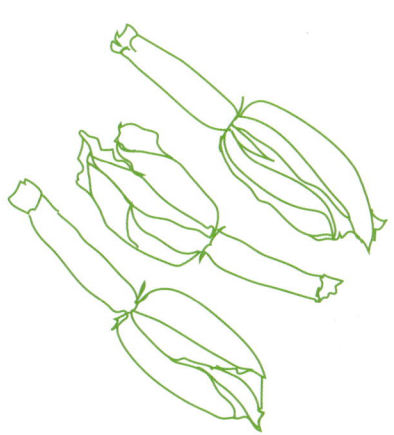

An Ebury Press book
Published by Random House Australia Pty Ltd
Level 3, 100 Pacific Highway, North Sydney NSW 2060
www.randomhouse.com.au

First published by Ebury Press in 2009

Copyright © Ed Halmagyi 2009

The moral right of the author has been asserted.

All rights reserved. No part of this book may be reproduced or transmitted by any person or entity, including internet search engines or retailers, in any form or by any means, electronic or mechanical, including photocopying (except under the statutory exceptions provisions of the Australian *Copyright Act 1968*), recording, scanning or by any information storage and retrieval system without the prior written permission of Random House Australia.

Addresses for companies within the Random House Group can be found at
www.randomhouse.com.au/offices

> National Library of Australia
> Cataloguing-in-Publication Entry
>
> Halmagyi, Ed.
> Dinner in 10.
>
> ISBN 978 1 74166 879 7 (pbk).
>
> Quick and easy cookery.
>
> 641.555

Cover and internal design by Jay Ryves/ Future Classic
Cover and internal photographs by Chris Jones
Illustrations by Leah Halmagyi
Printed and bound by 1010 Printing International Limited

10 9 8 7 6 5 4 3 2 1